Copyright Notice: © 2024 Keo Rithy. All rights reserved. Unauthorized reproduction or distribution of the content within this activity book is prohibited by copyright law.

All Rights Reserve: All rights to the content including images, text, and design of this activity book, are reserved by the copyright holder. Users are prohibited from reproducing, distributing, or modifying the content without explicit authorization.

Terms of Use: This activity book is intended for personal use only. Commercial use, sharing, or selling copies of this activity book is strictly prohibited. Unauthorized distribution or modification of the content is a violation of the copyright holder's rights.

Disclaimers: The publisher and author of his activity book disclaim any liability or responsibility for errors, inaccuracies, or damages that may arise from the use of this book. Users are responsible for using this activity book with appropriate supervision and care.

FULL PICTURE

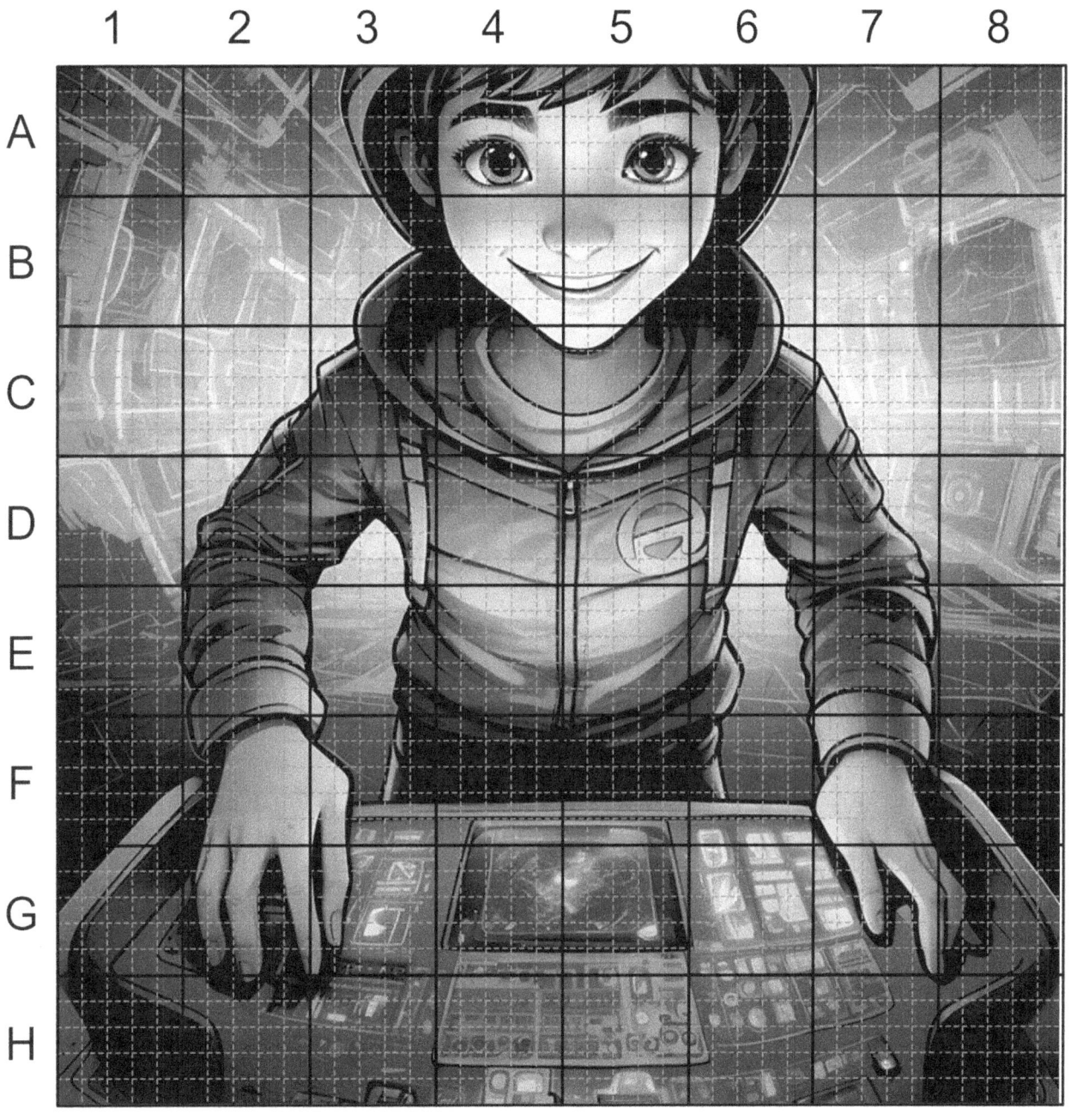

STEP #1: DRAW A1-D4

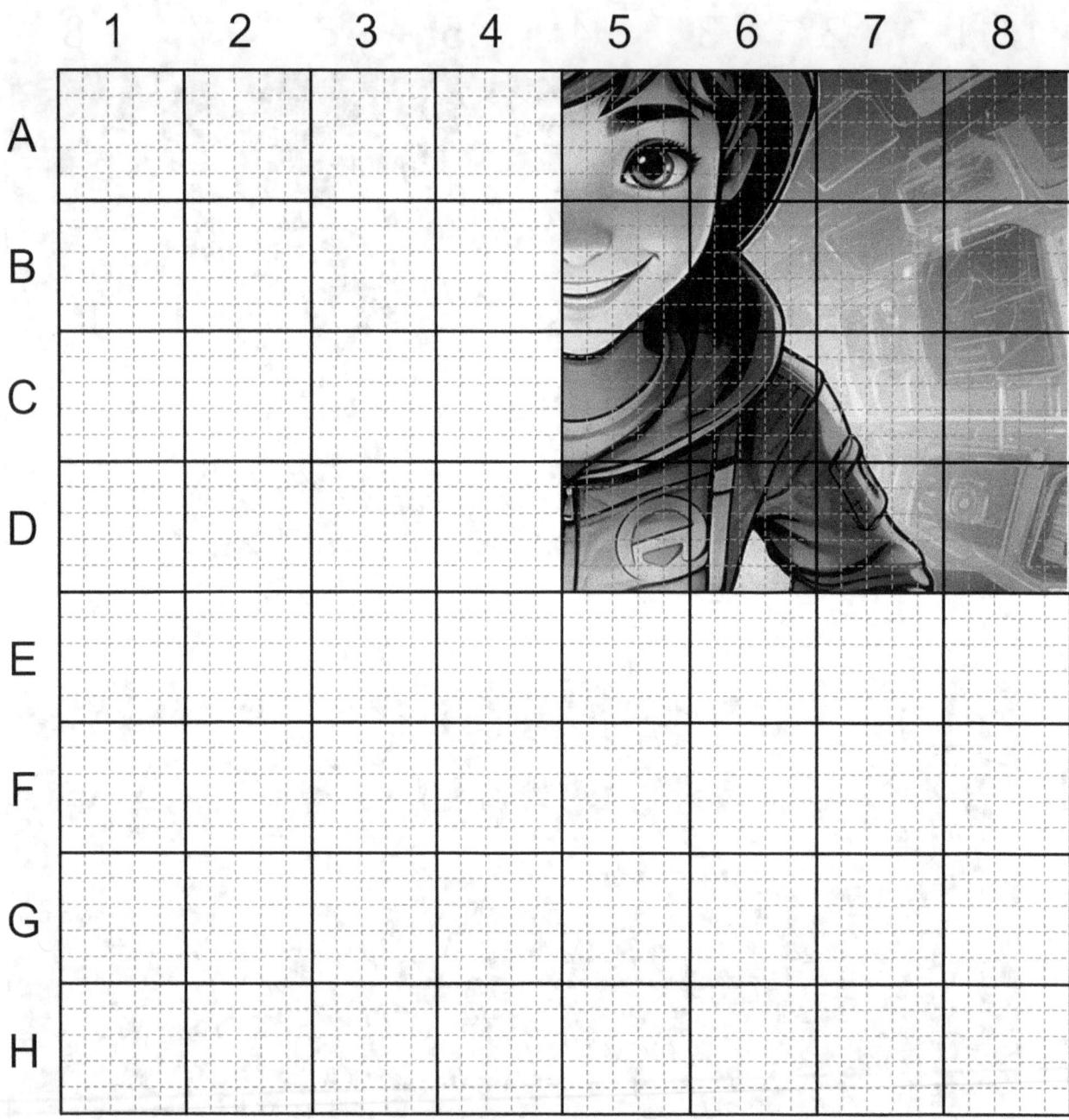

STEP #2: DRAW E1-H4

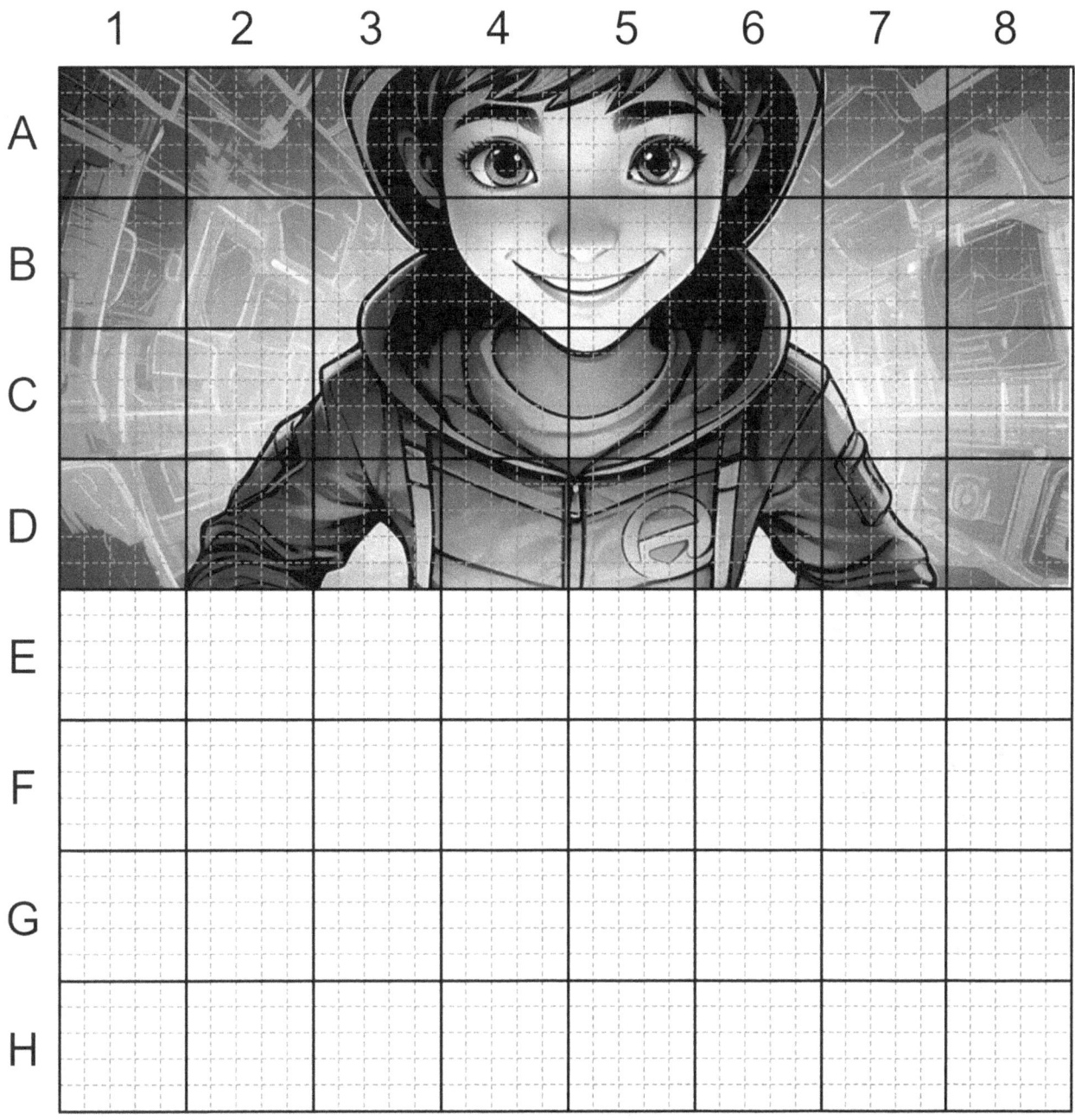

STEP #3: DRAW E5-H8

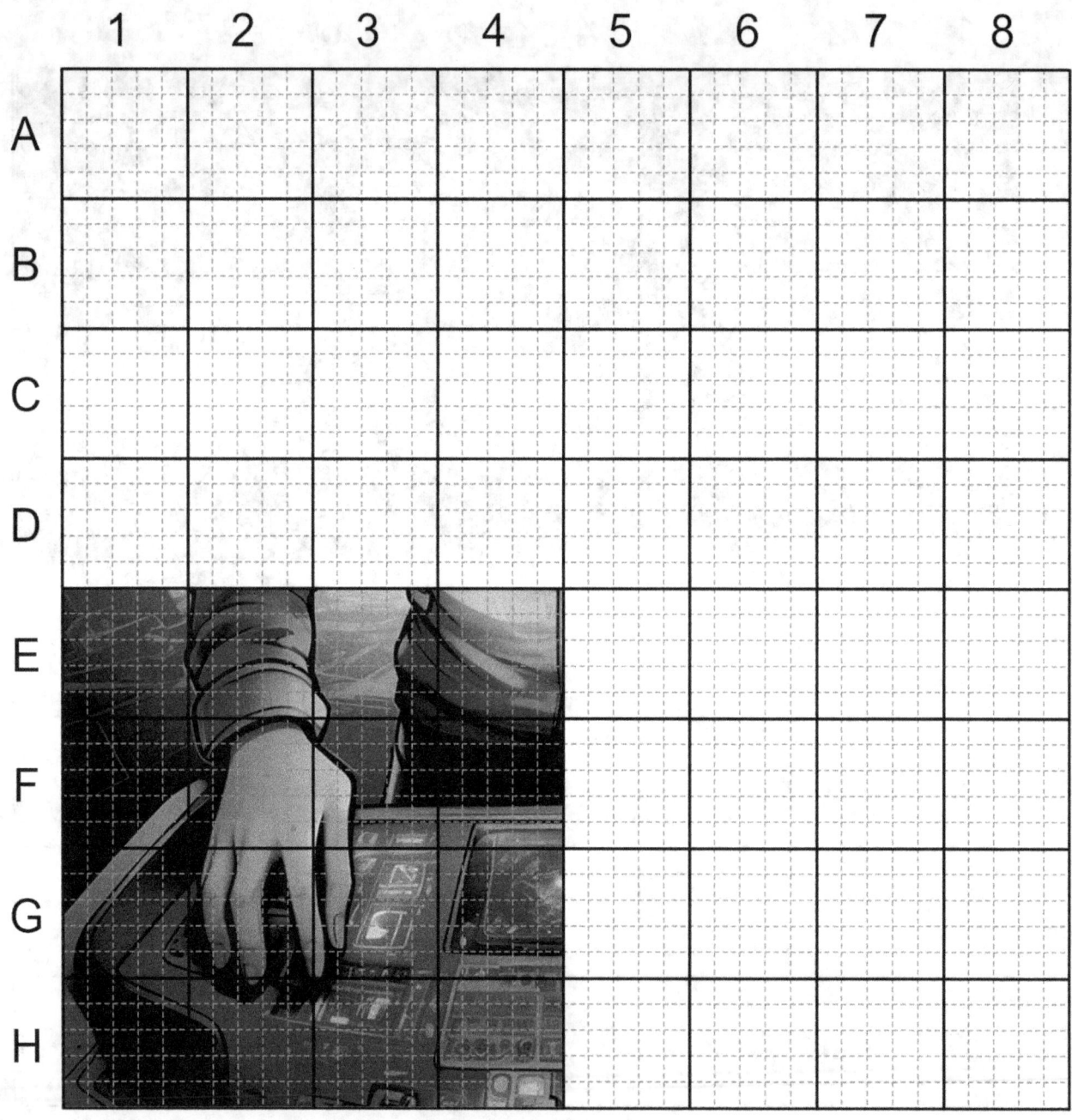

STEP #4: DRAW A5-D8

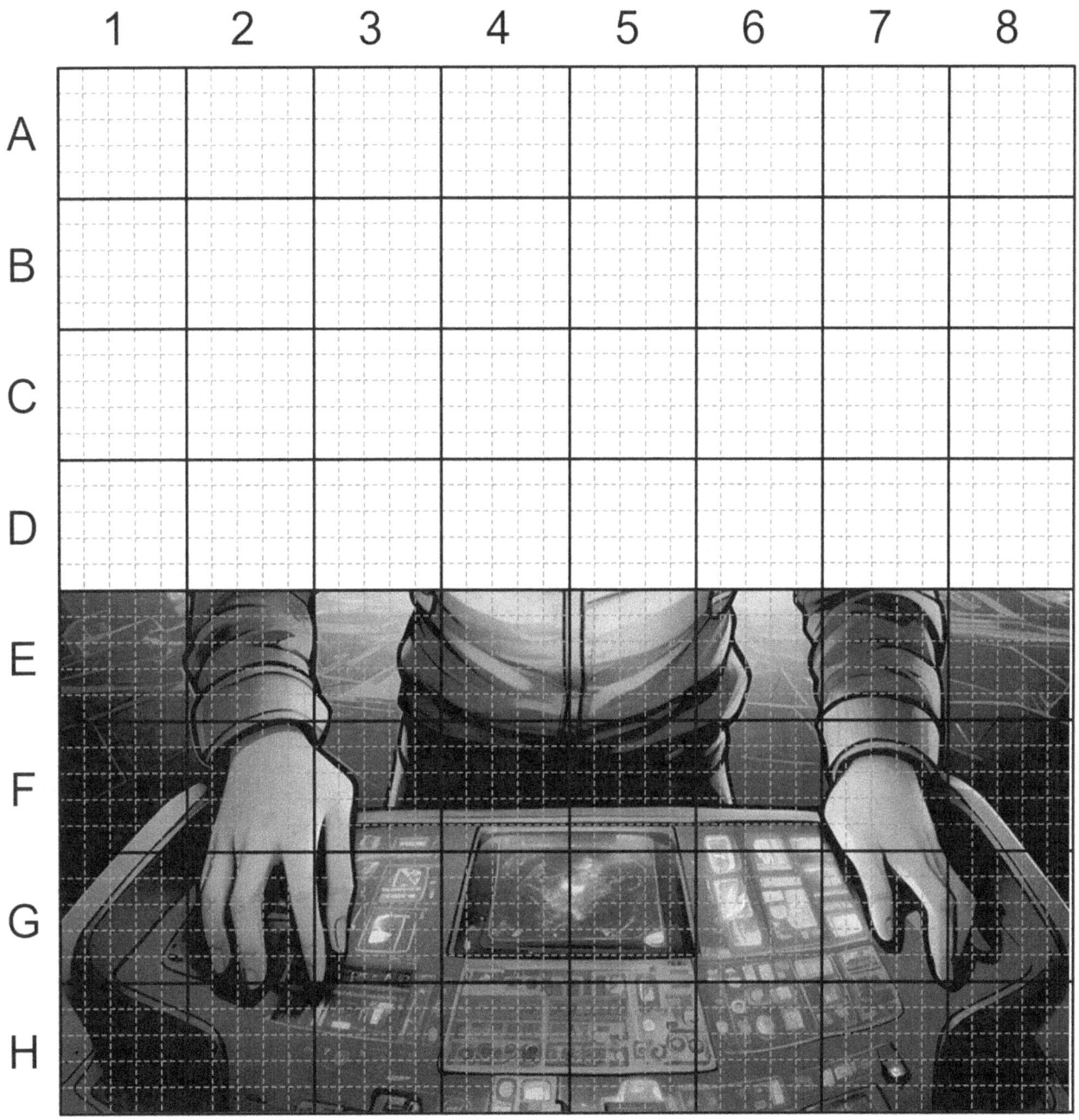

FINAL PICTURE

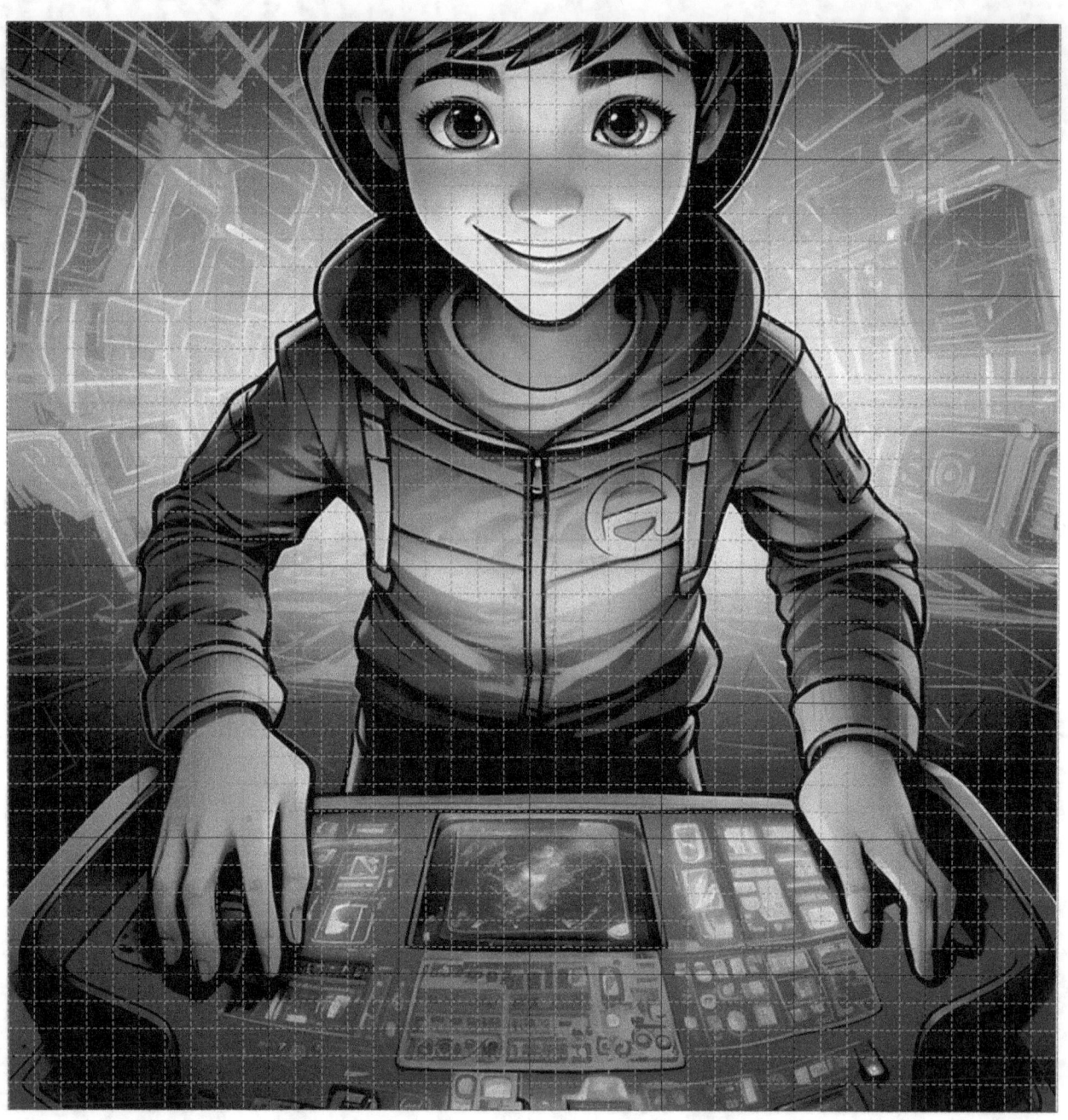

FULL PICTURE

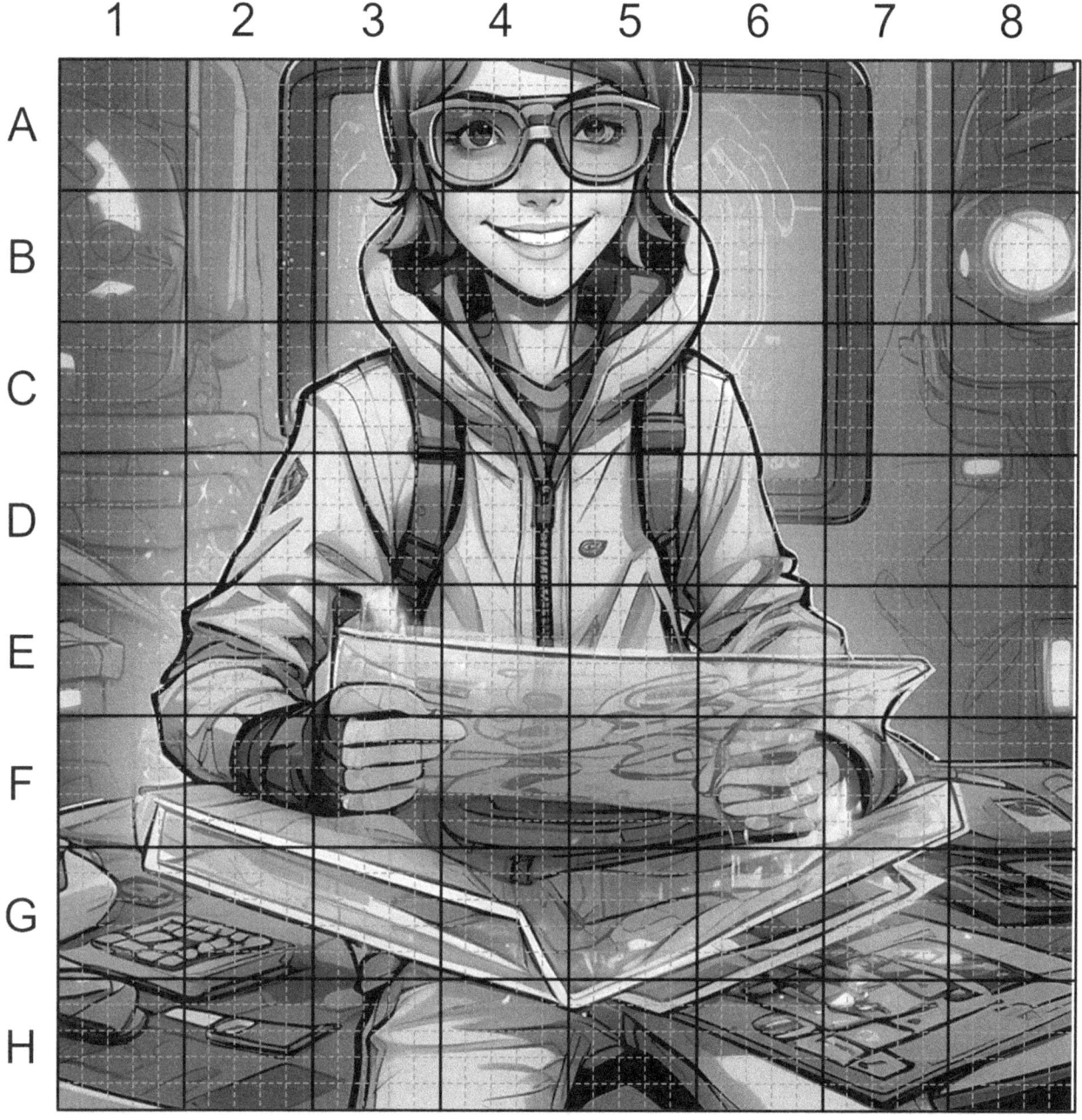

STEP #1: DRAW A1-D4

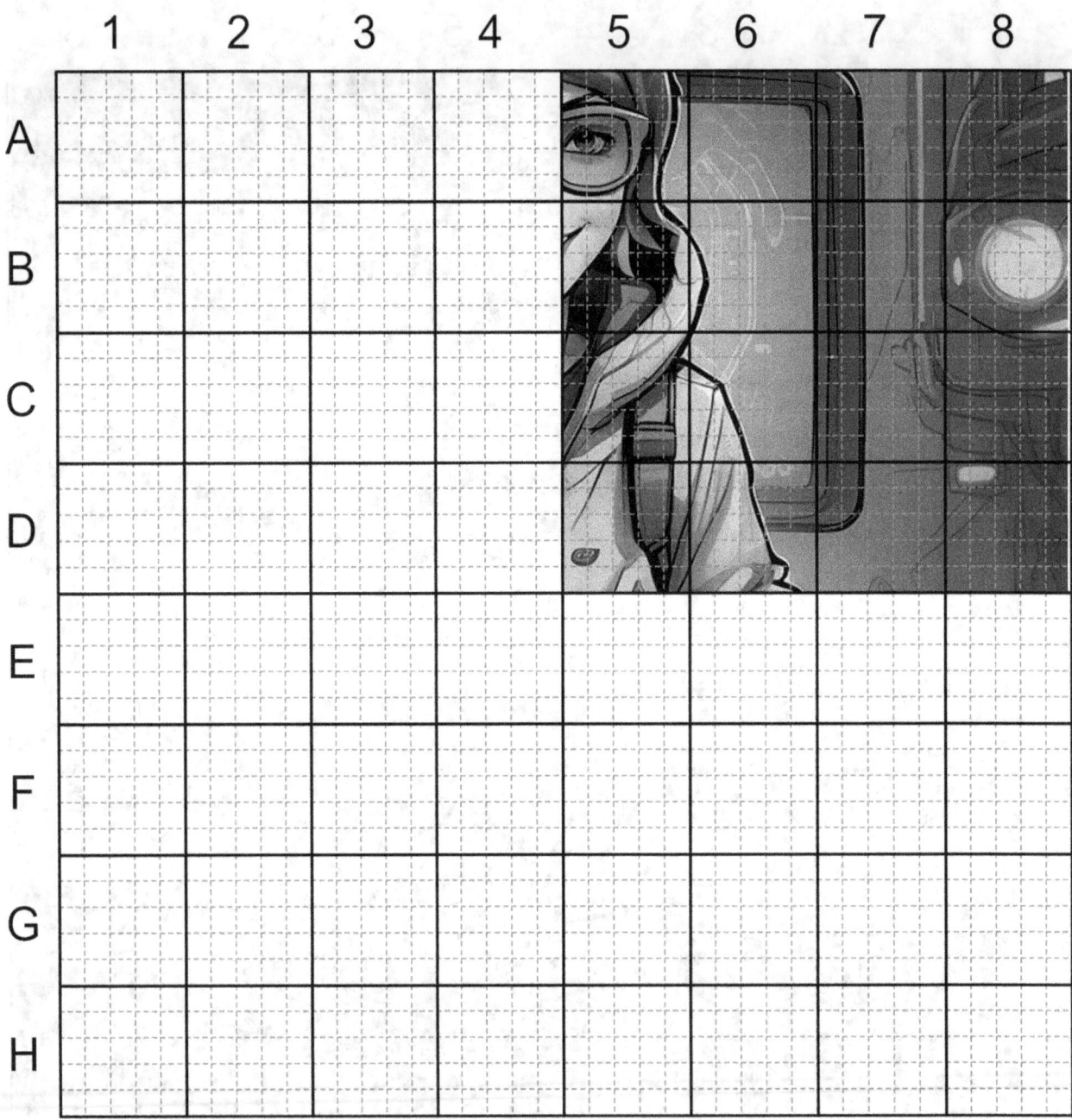

STEP #2: DRAW E1-H4

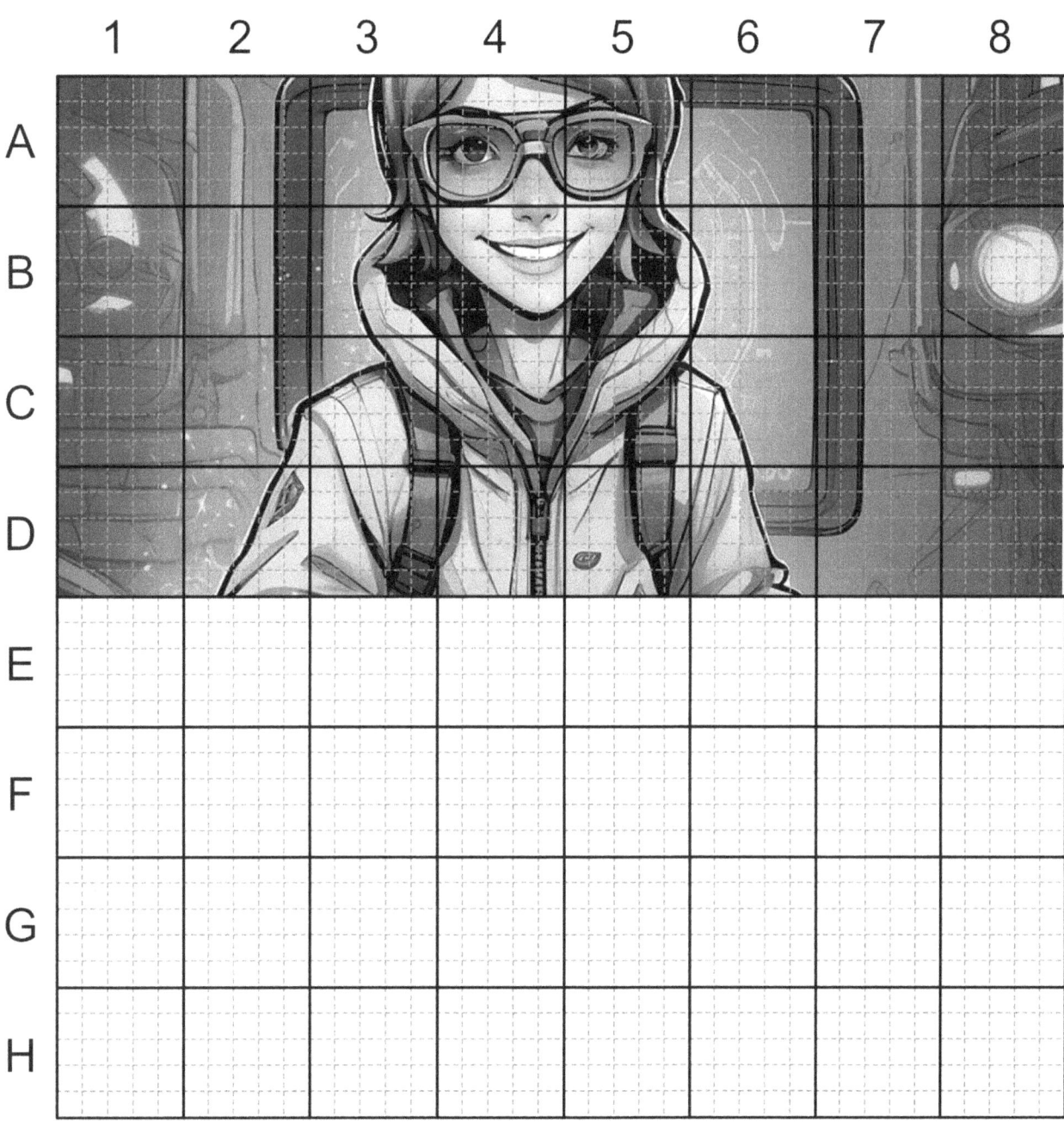

STEP #3: DRAW E5-H8

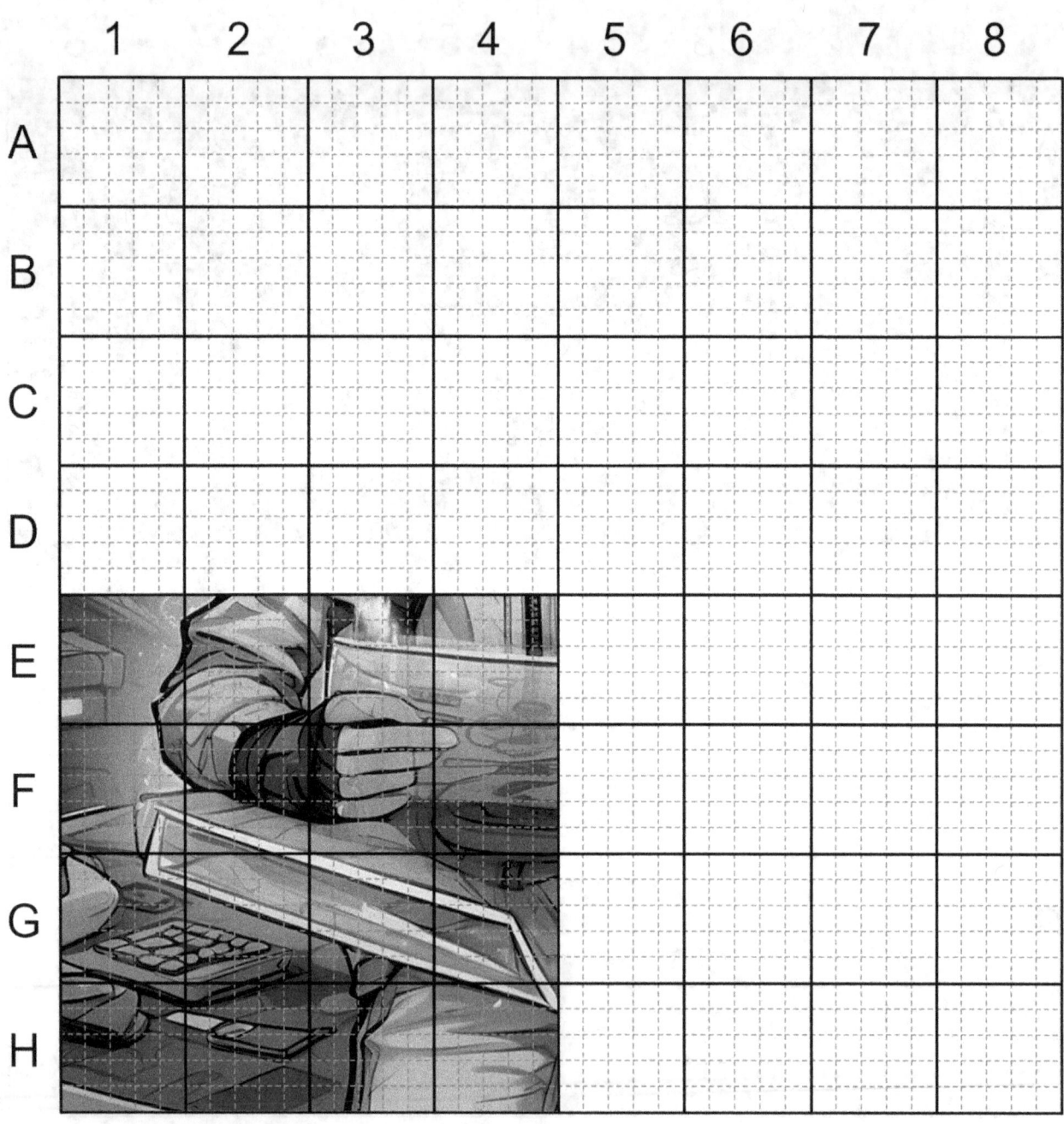

STEP #4: DRAW A5-D8

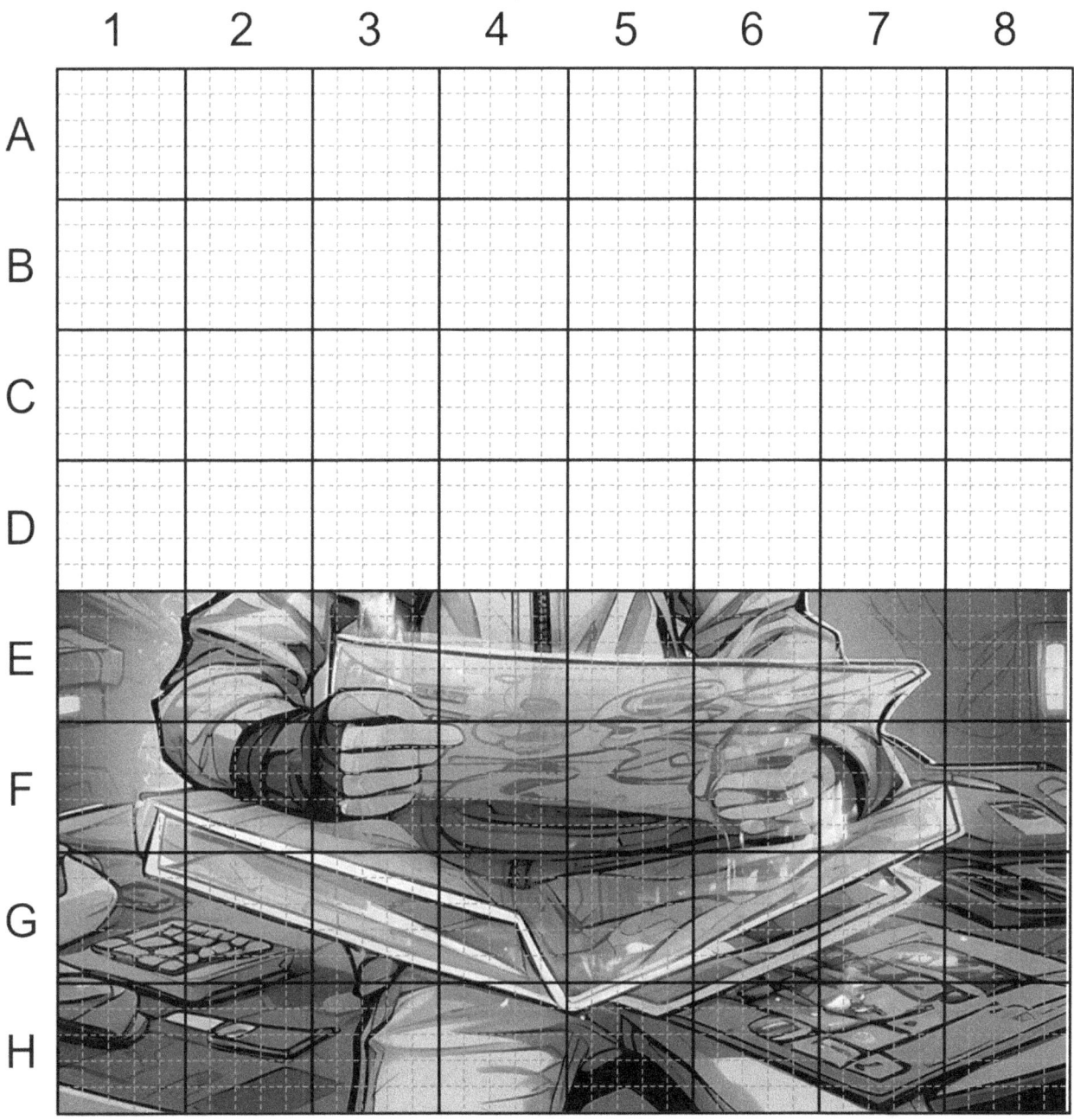

FINAL PICTURE

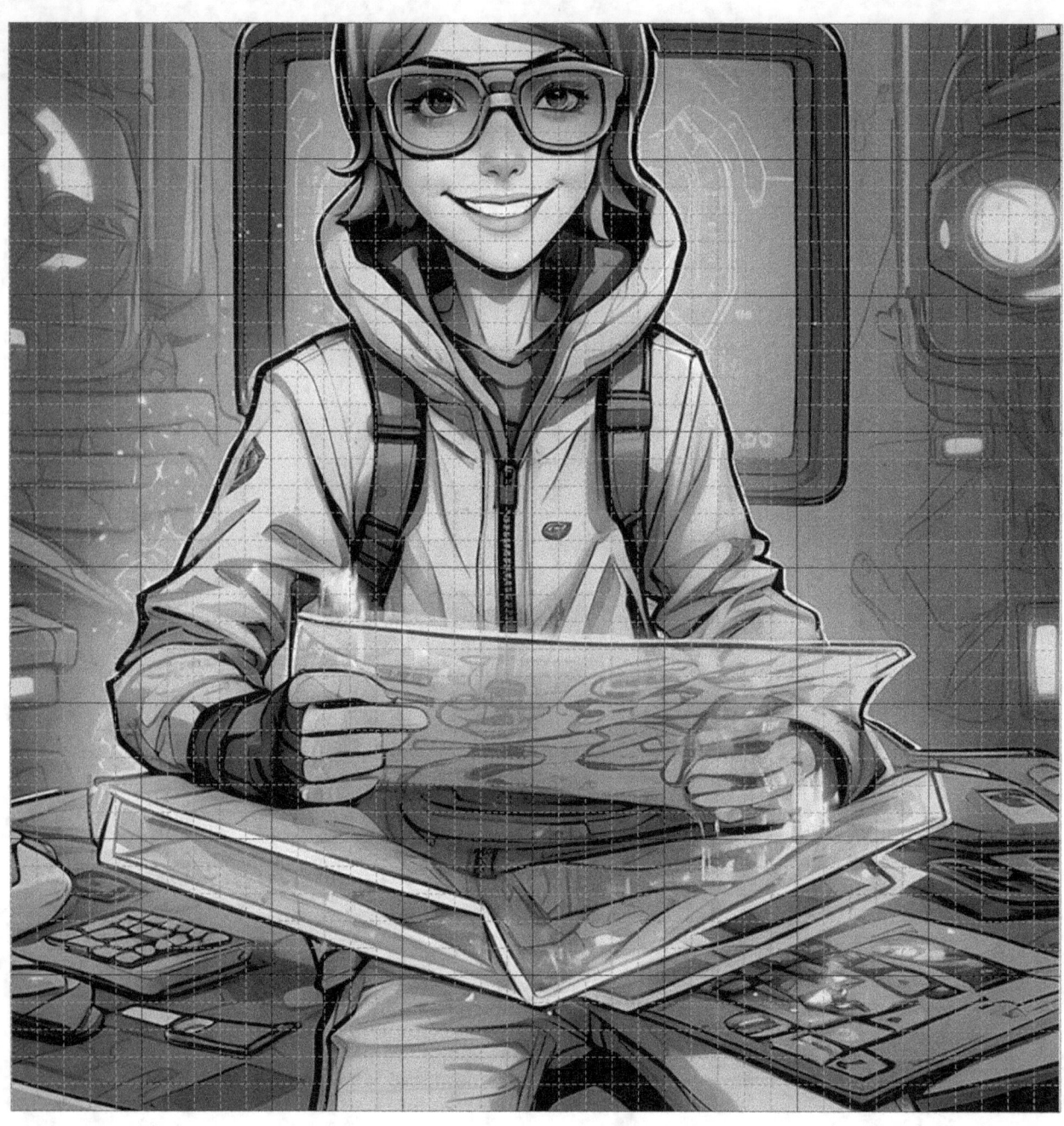

FULL PICTURE

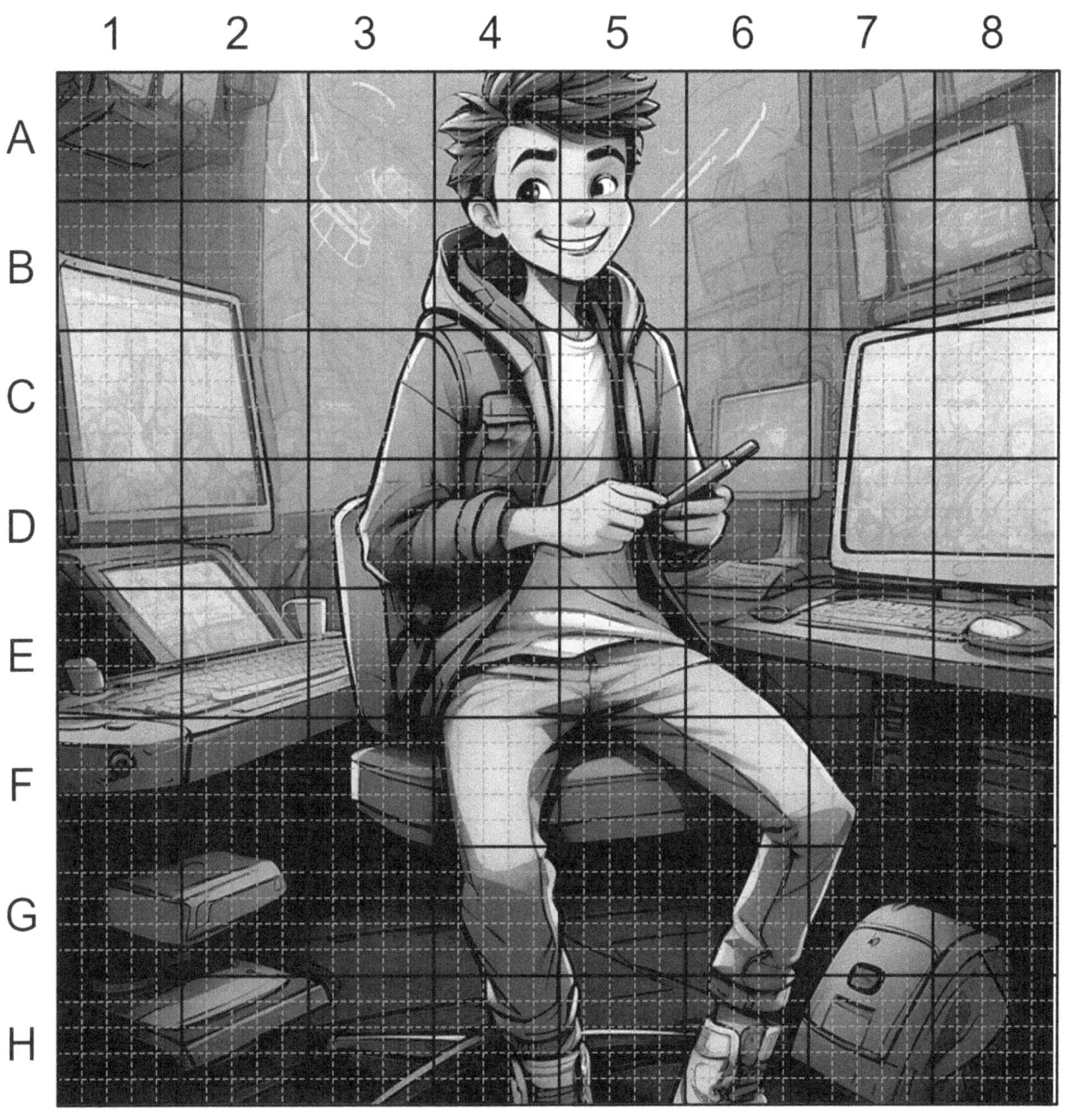

STEP #1: DRAW A1-D4

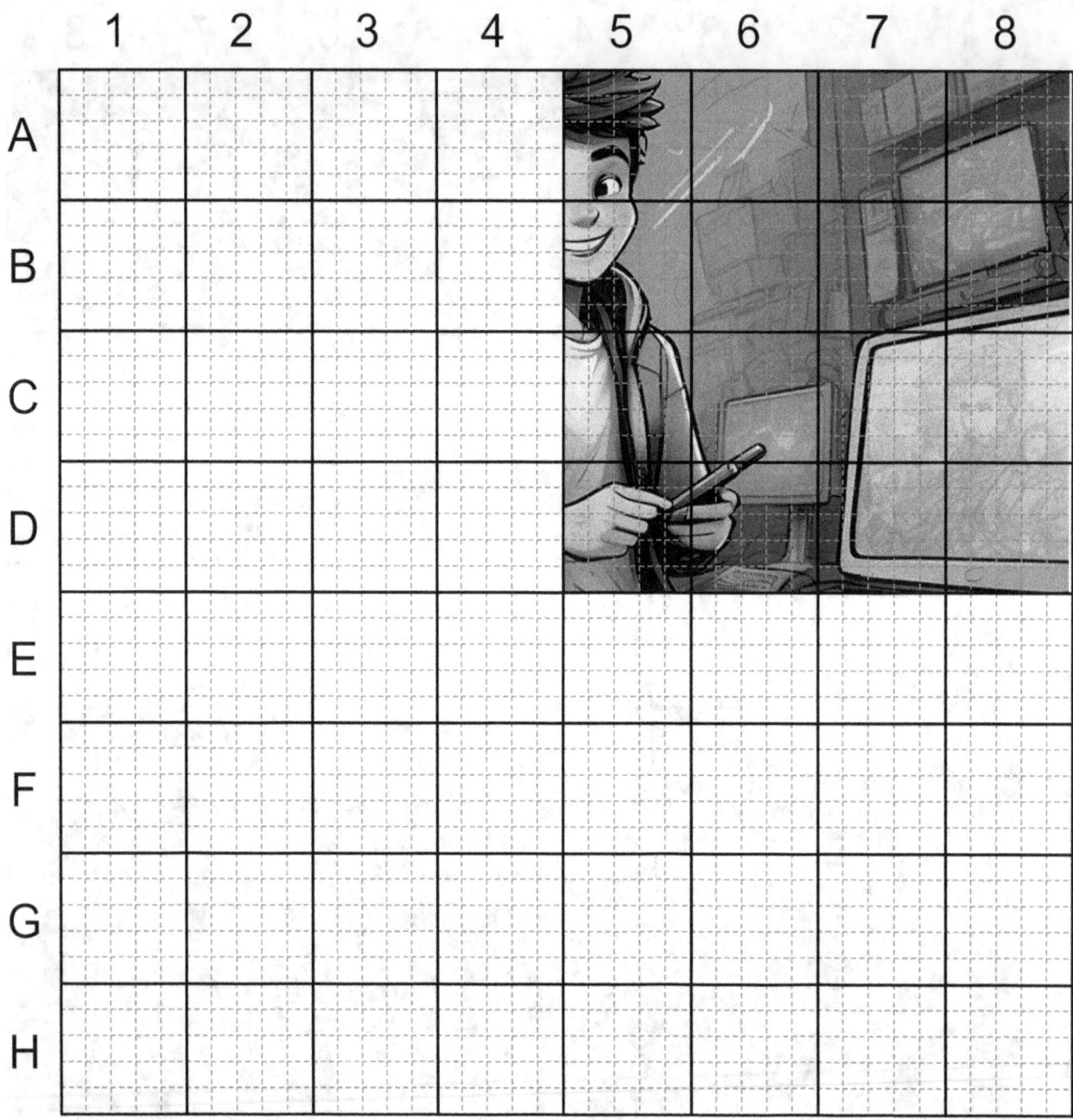

STEP #2: DRAW E1-H4

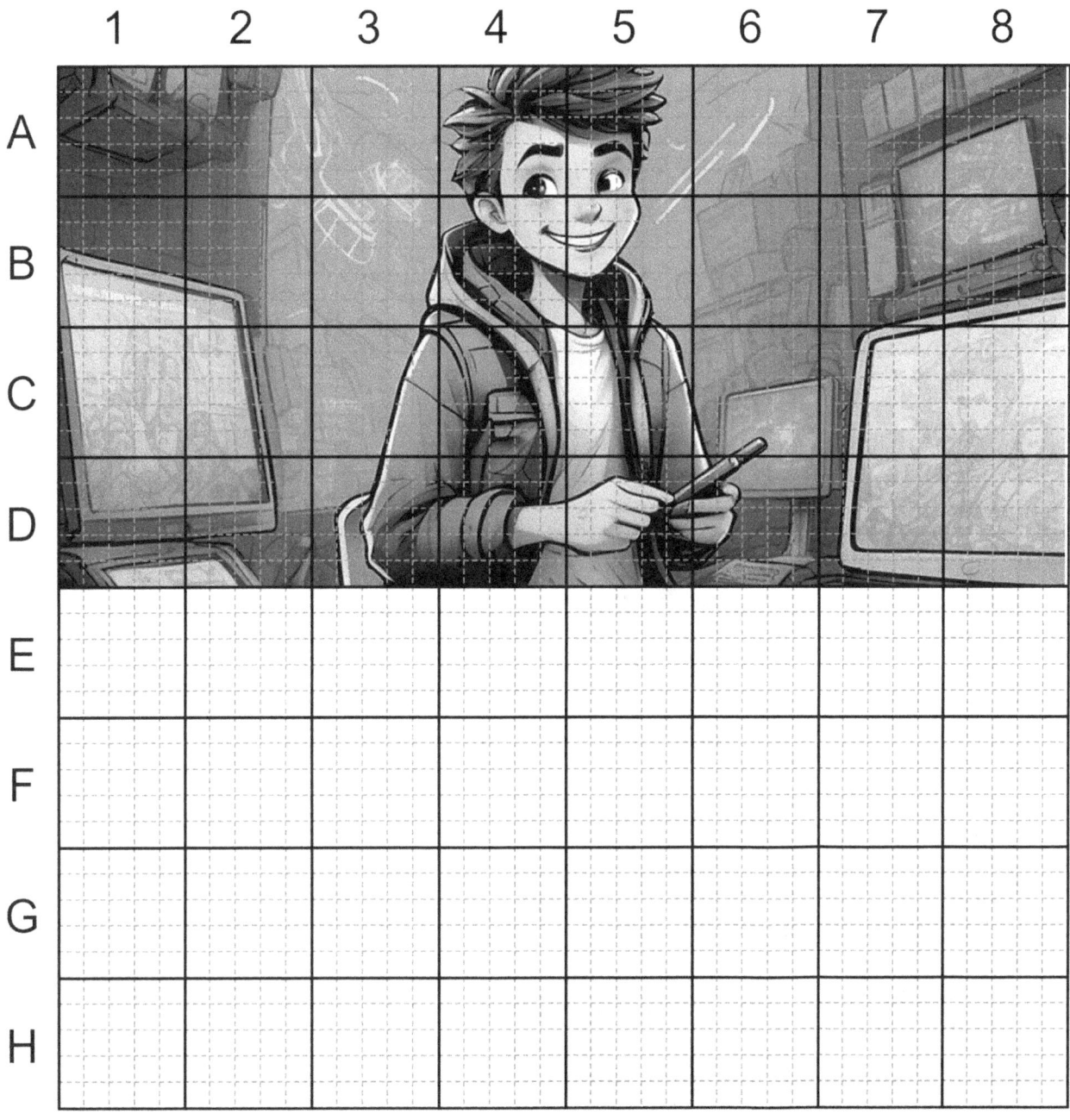

STEP #3: DRAW E5-H8

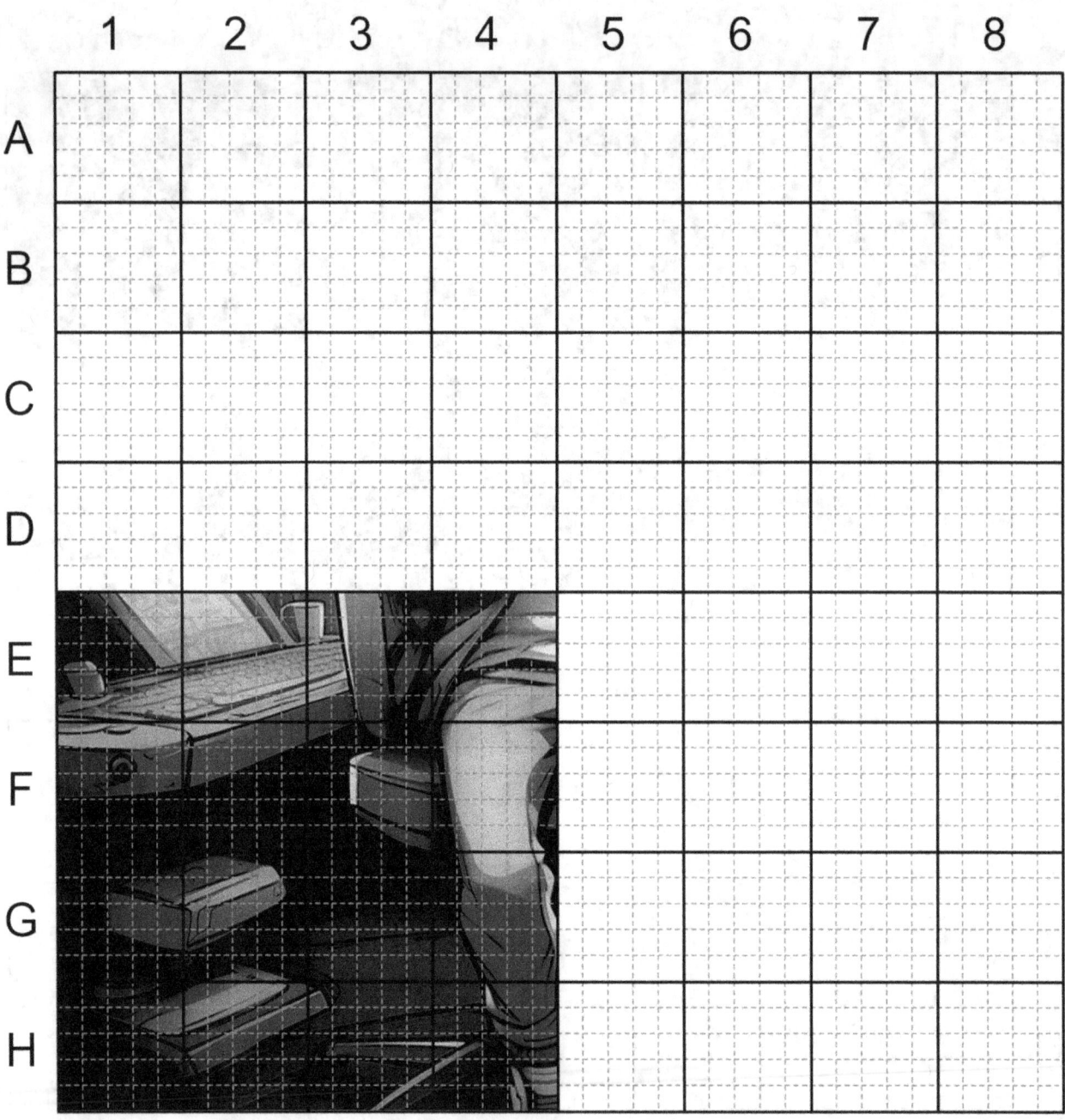

STEP #4: DRAW A5-D8

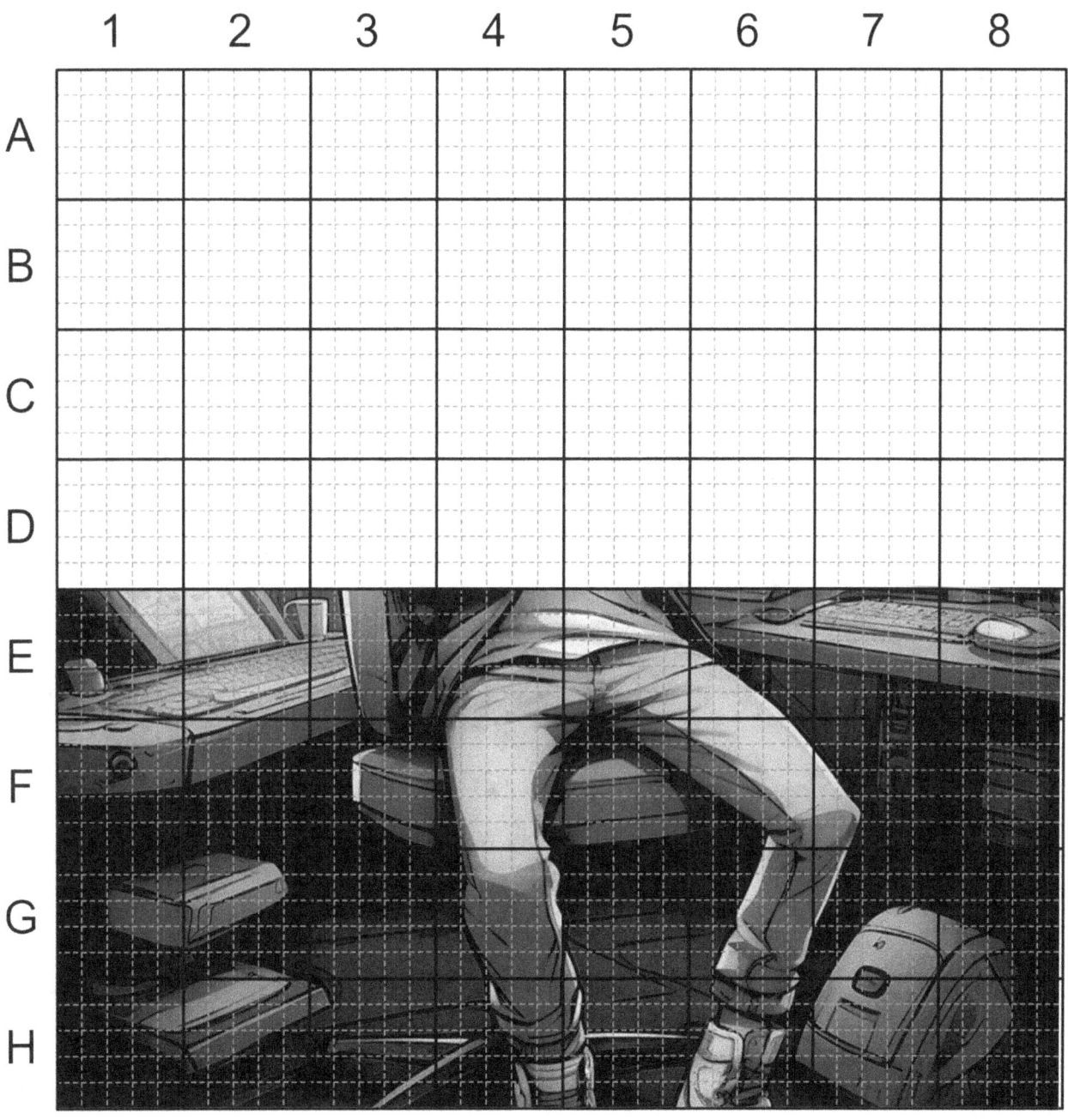

FINAL PICTURE

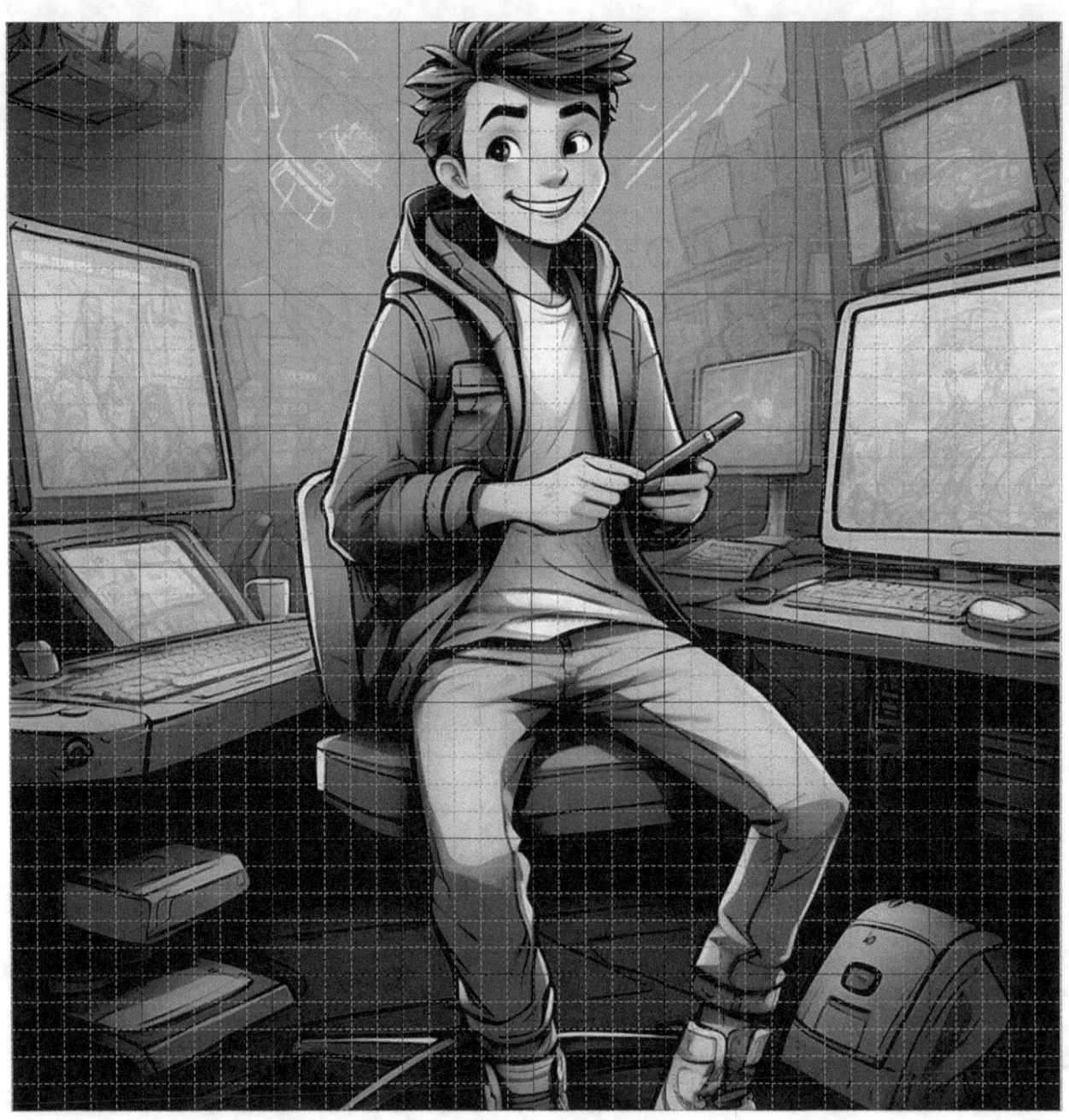

FULL PICTURE

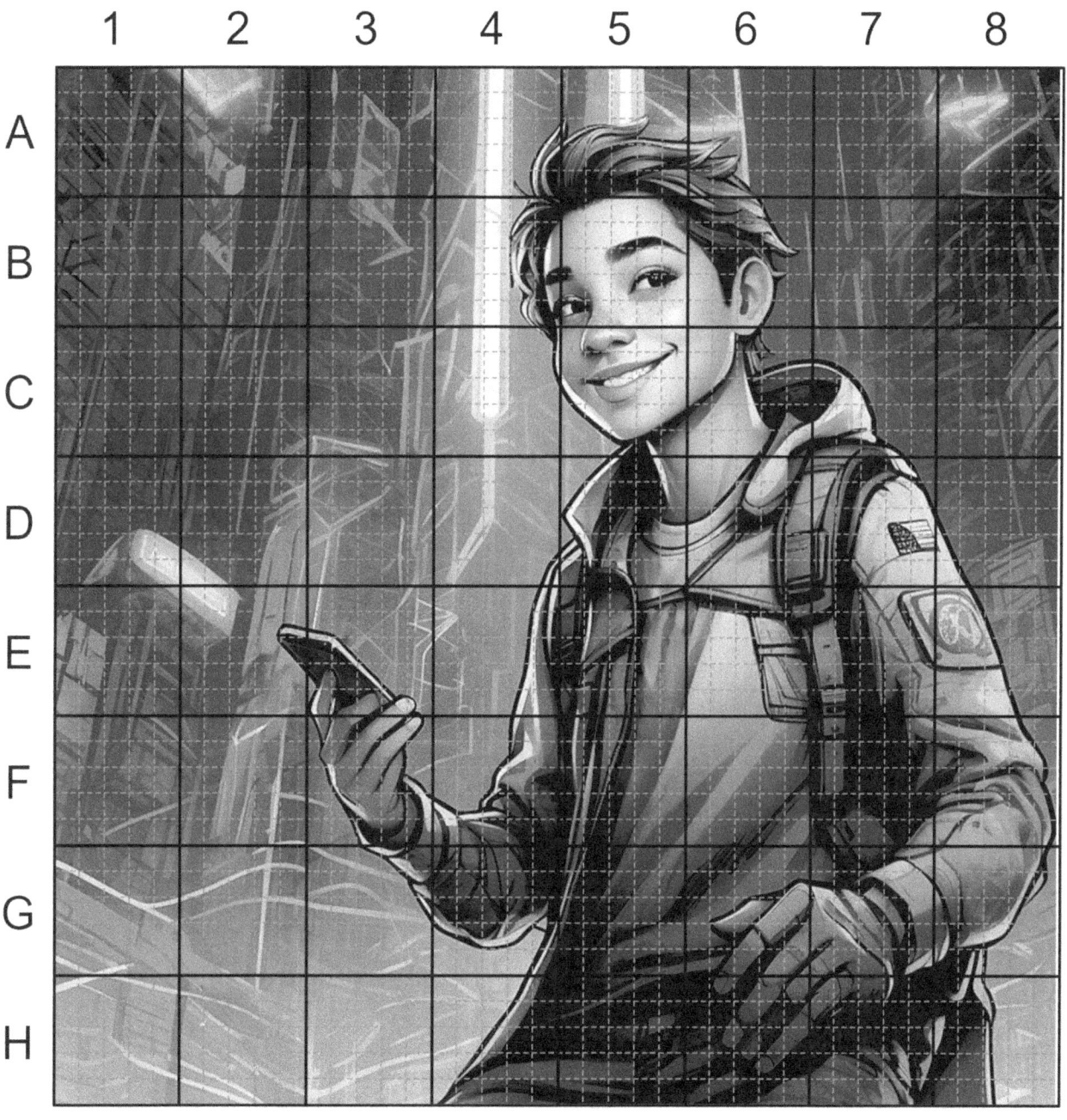

STEP #1: DRAW A1-D4

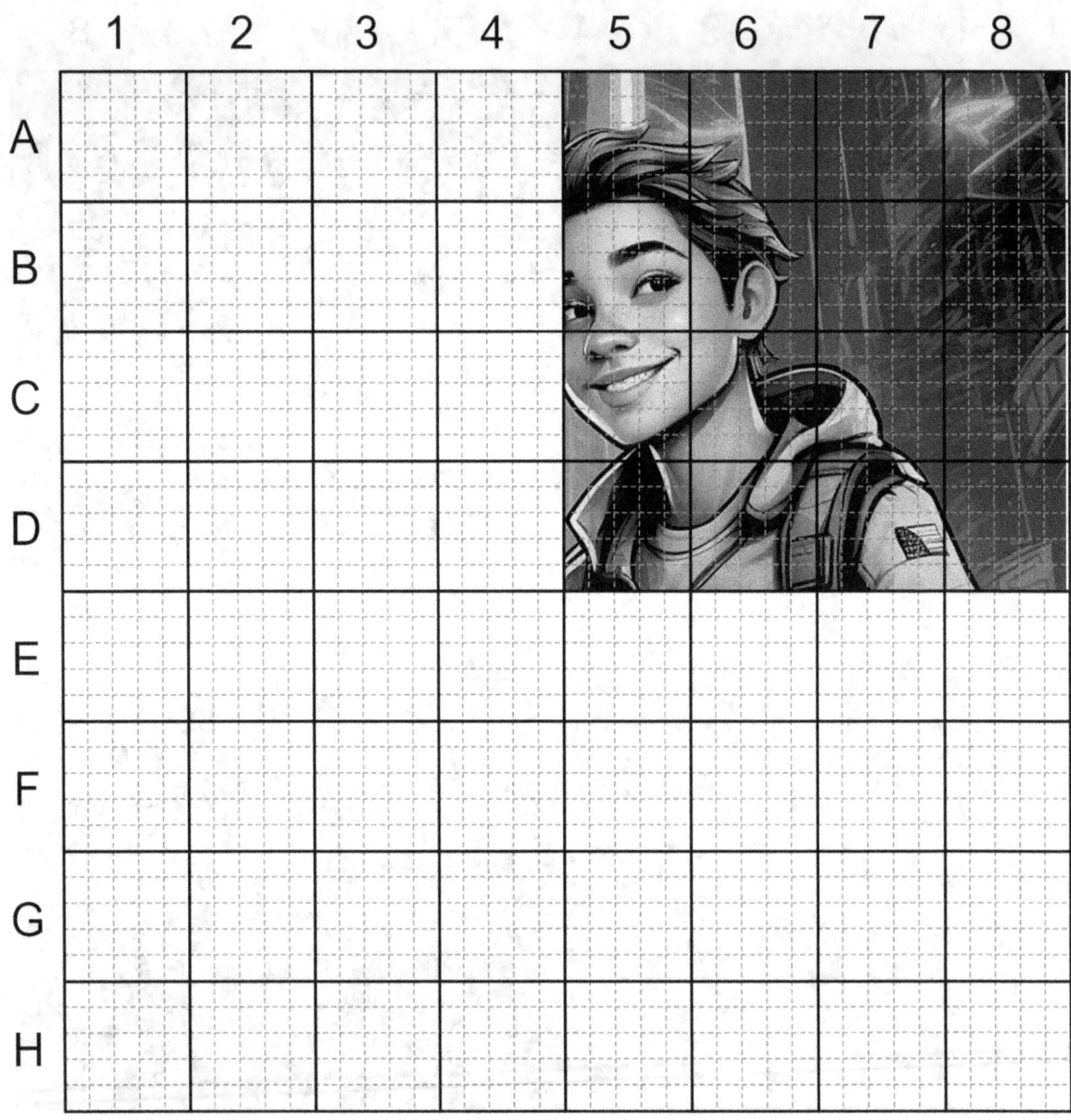

STEP #2: DRAW E1-H4

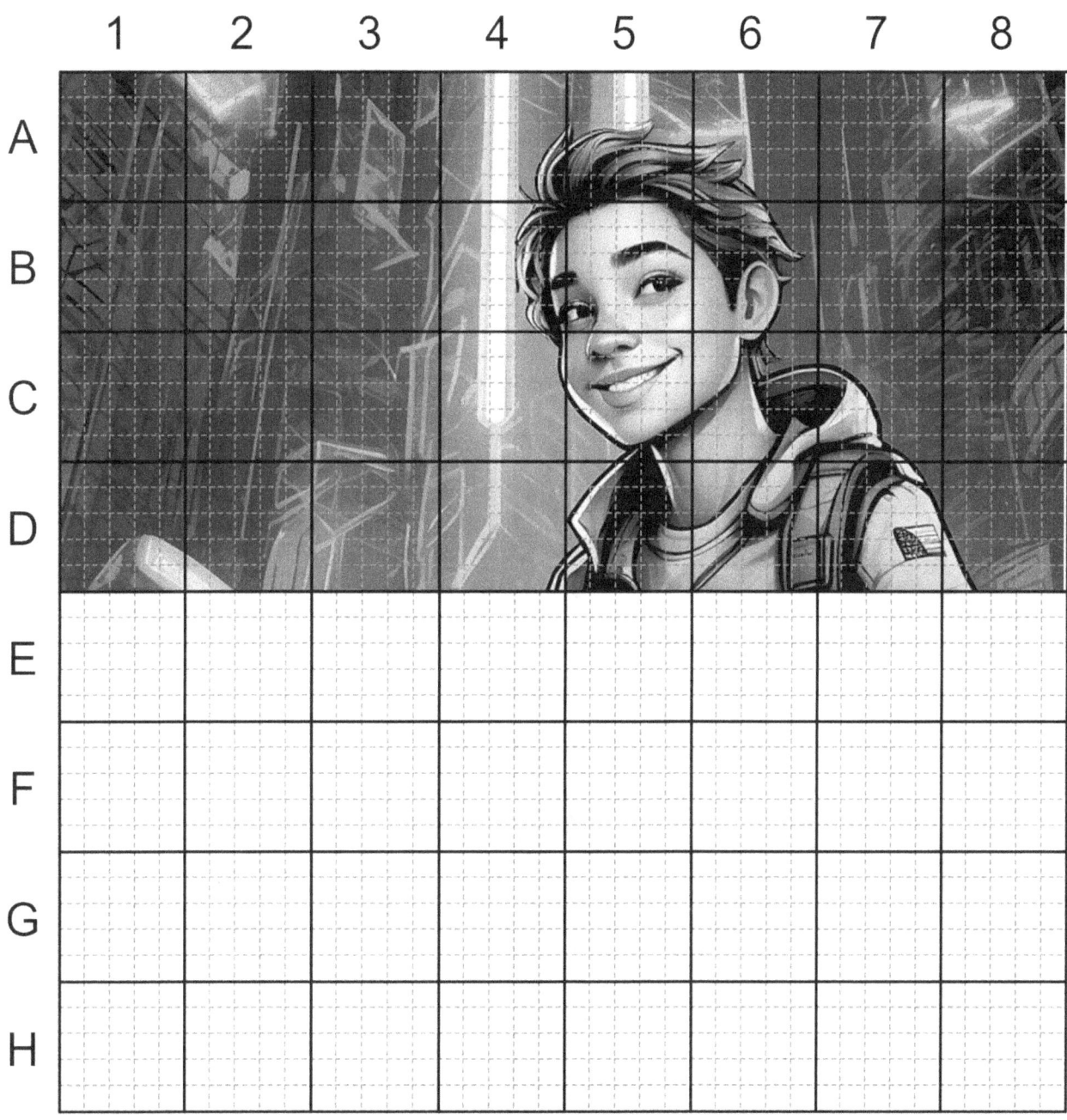

STEP #3: DRAW E5-H8

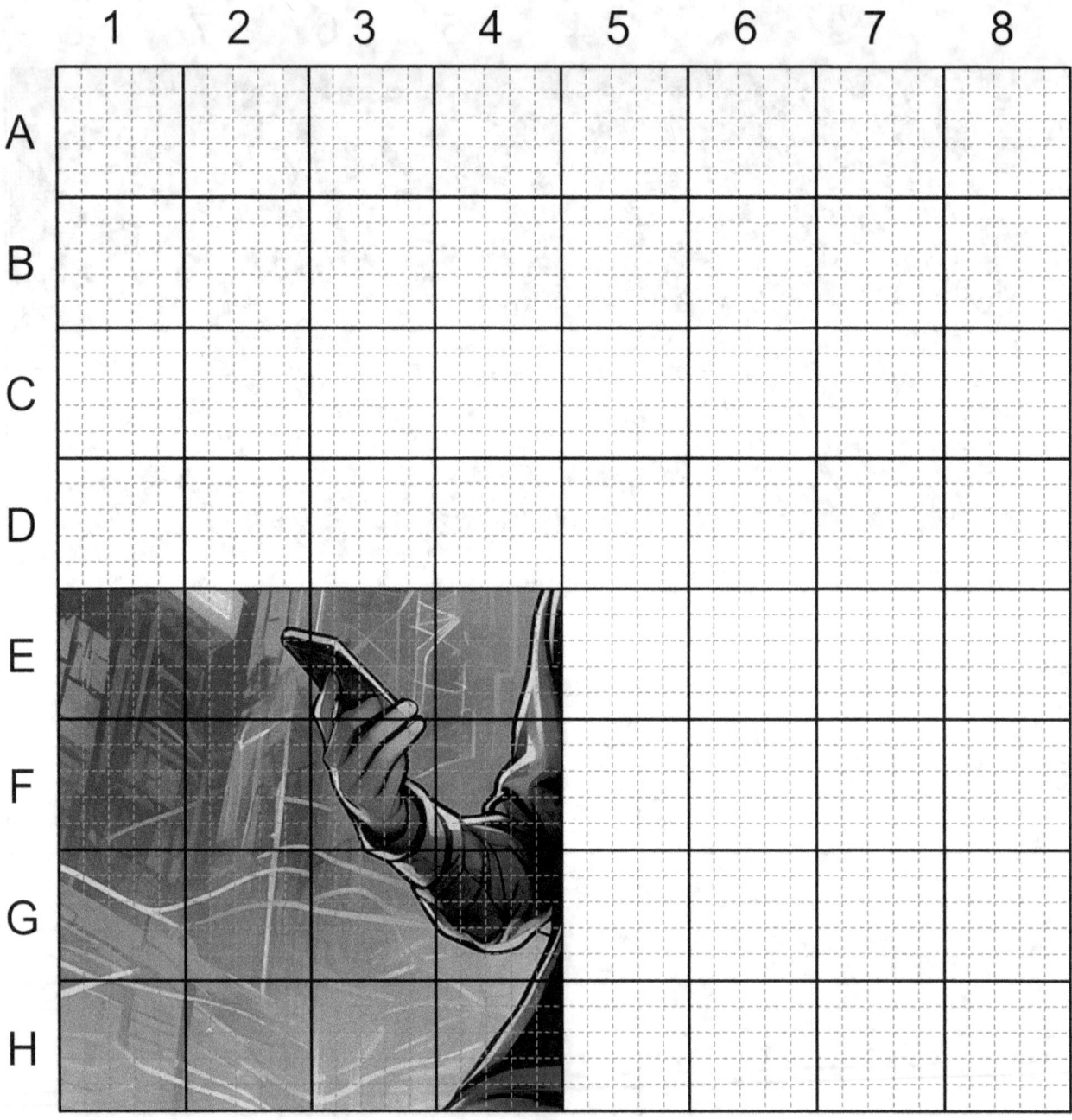

STEP #4: DRAW A5-D8

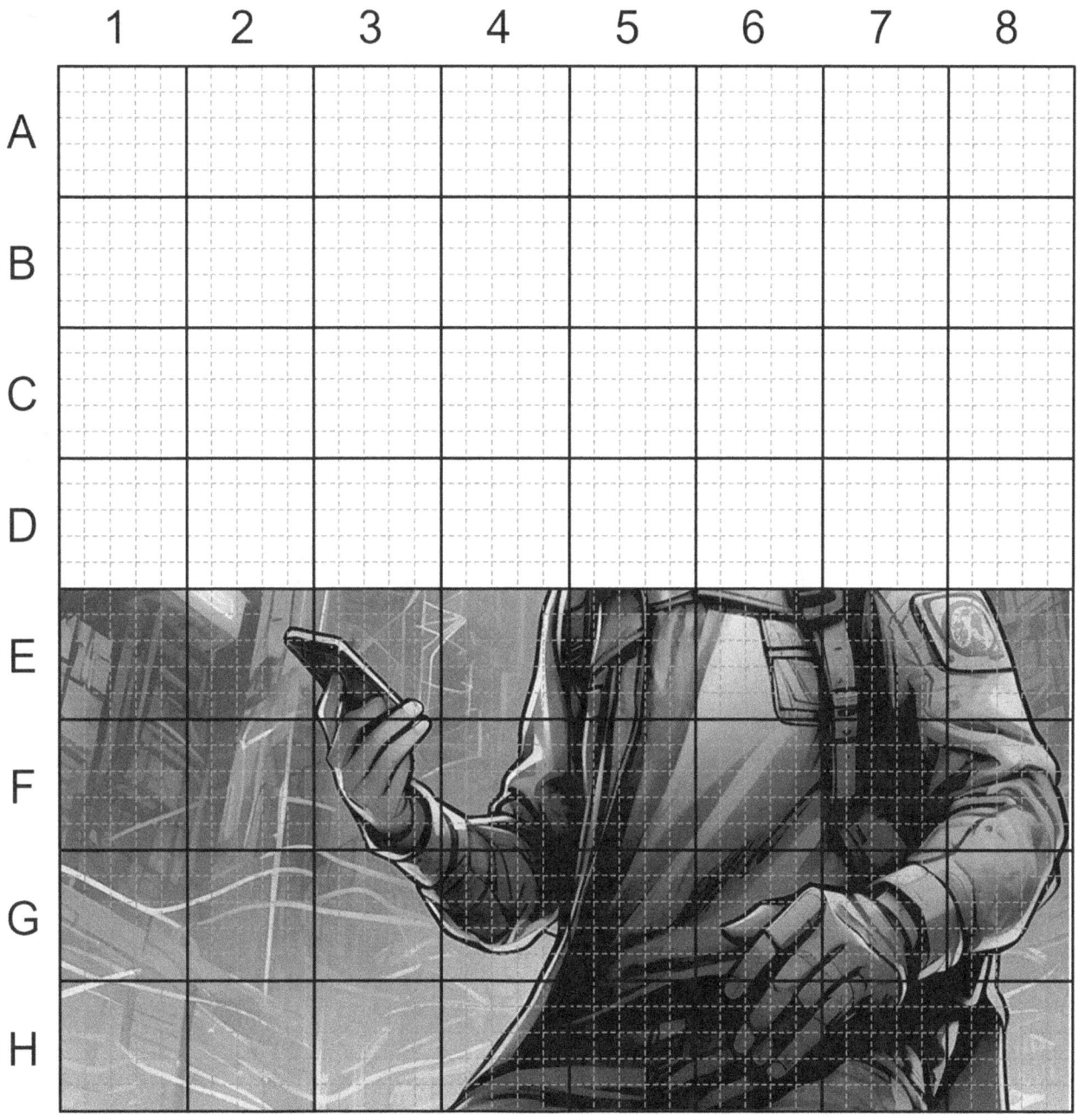

FINAL PICTURE

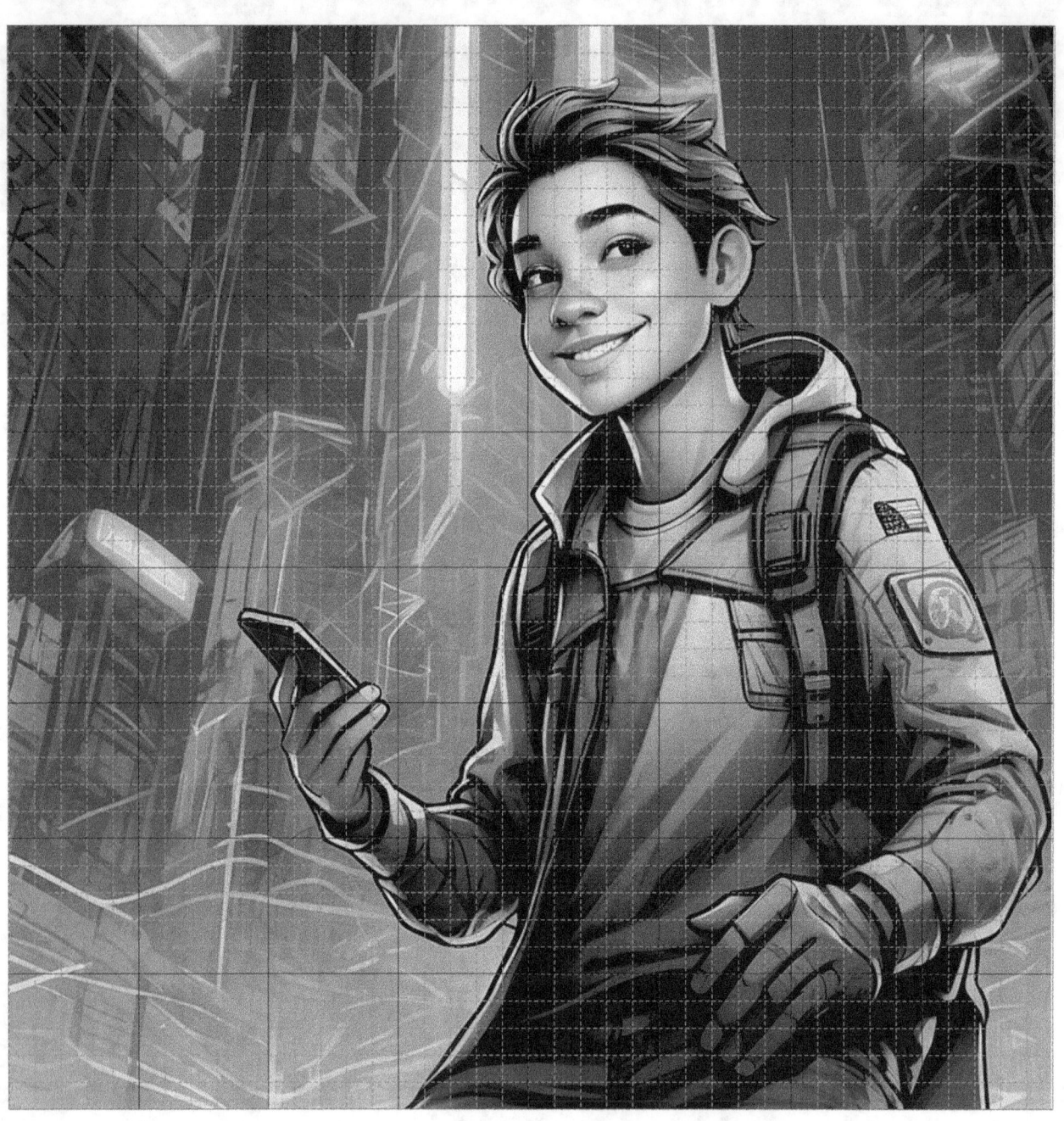

FULL PICTURE

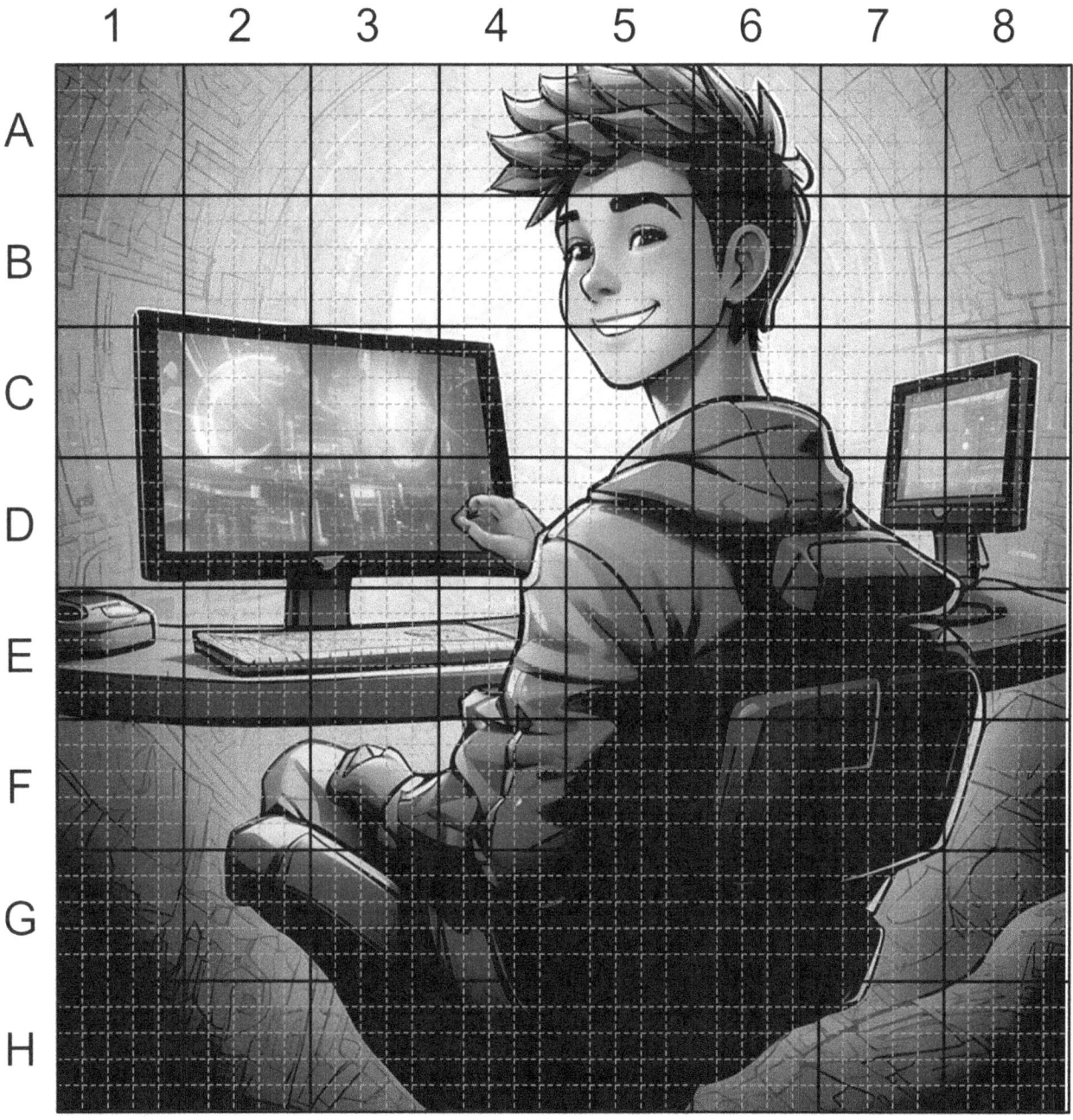

STEP #1: DRAW A1-D4

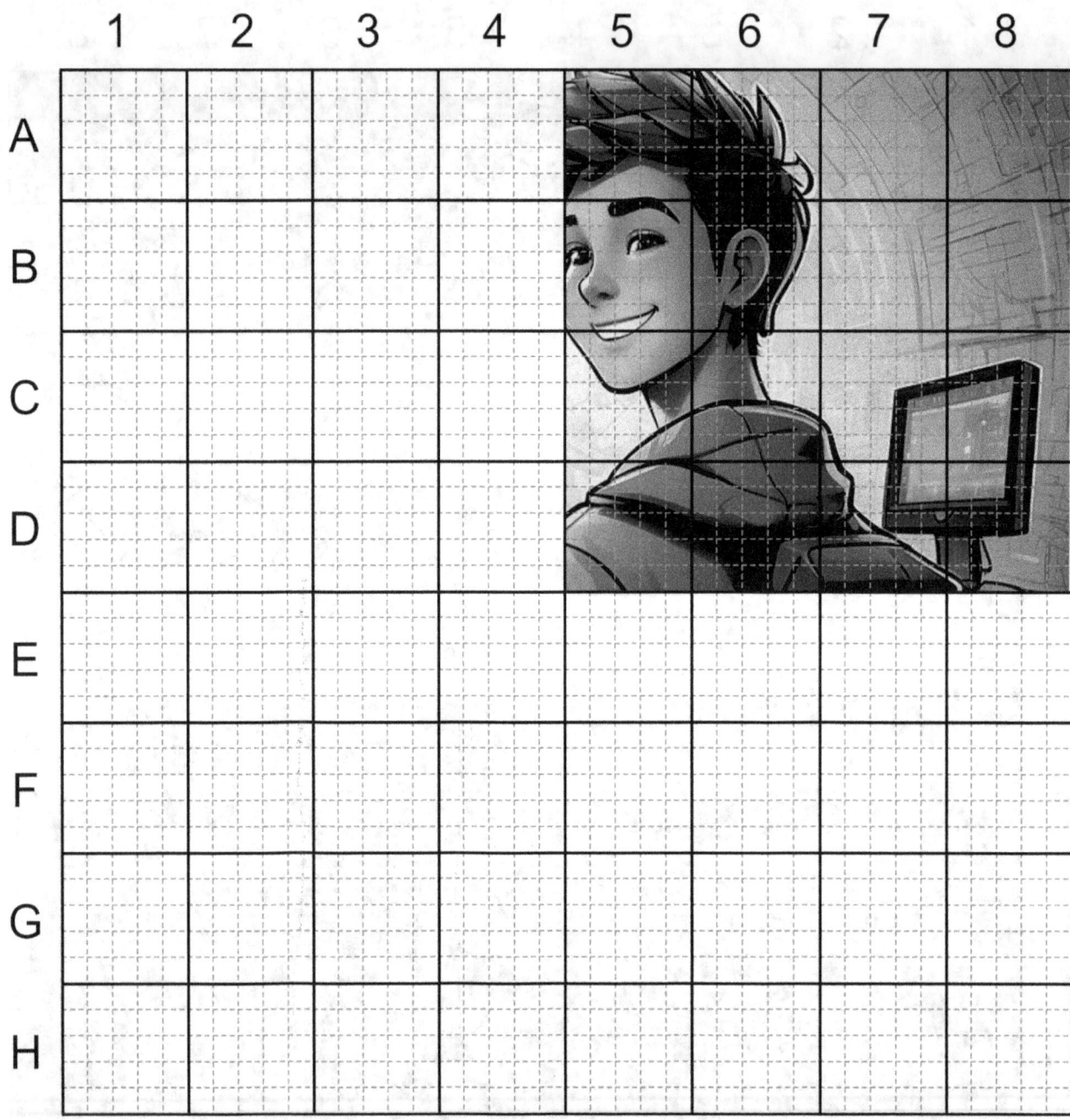

STEP #2: DRAW E1-H4

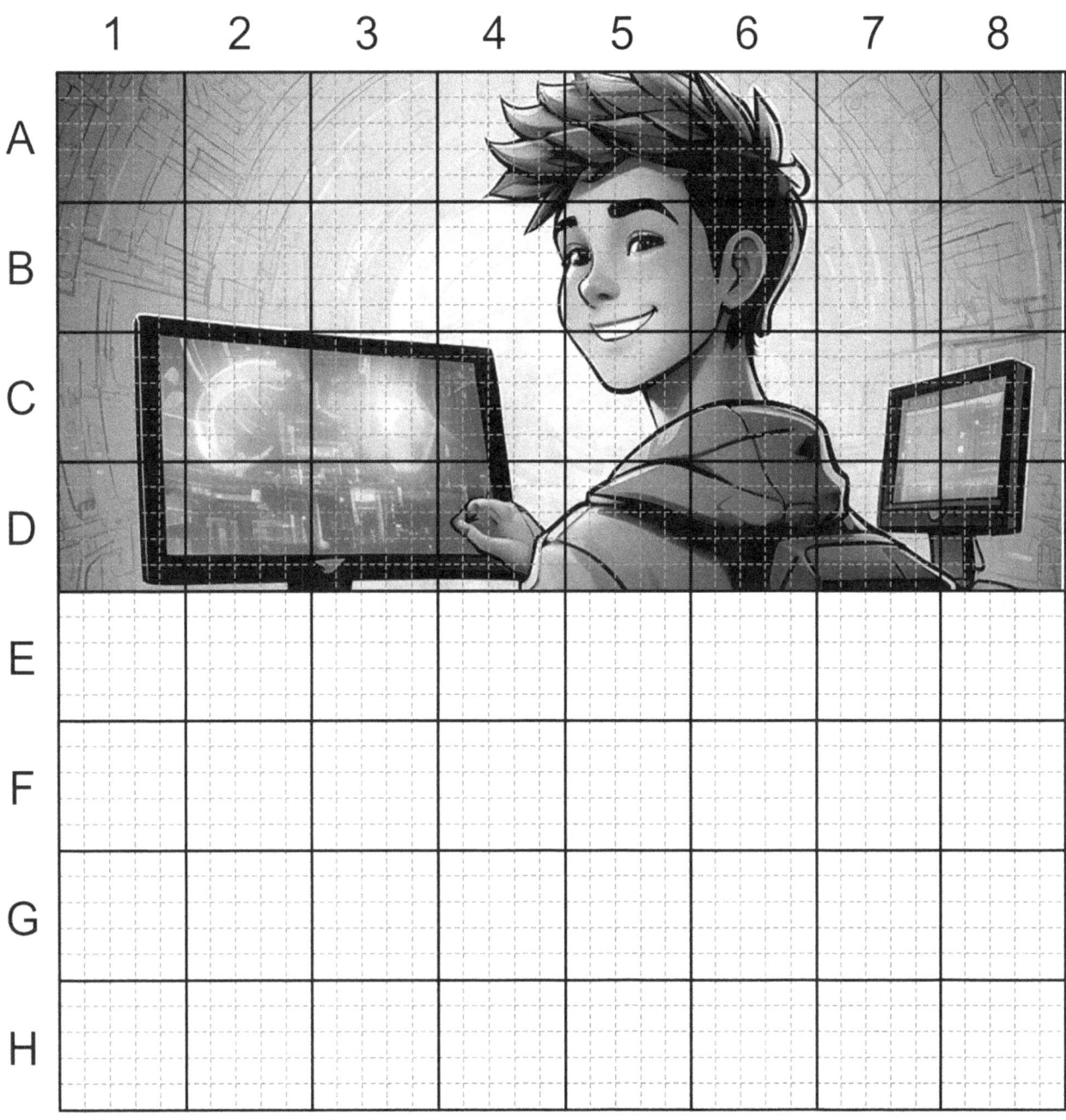

STEP #3: DRAW E5-H8

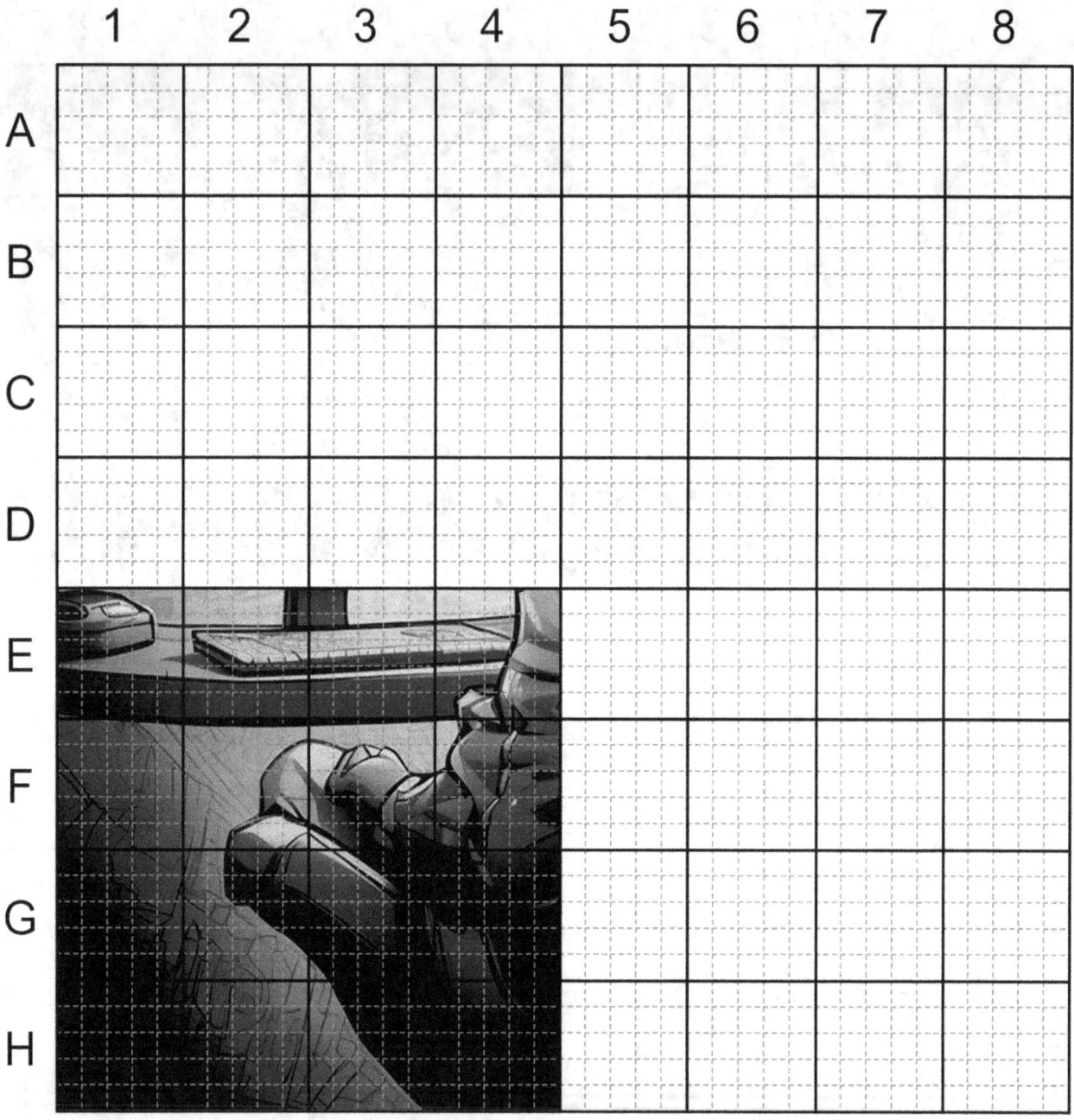

STEP #4: DRAW A5-D8

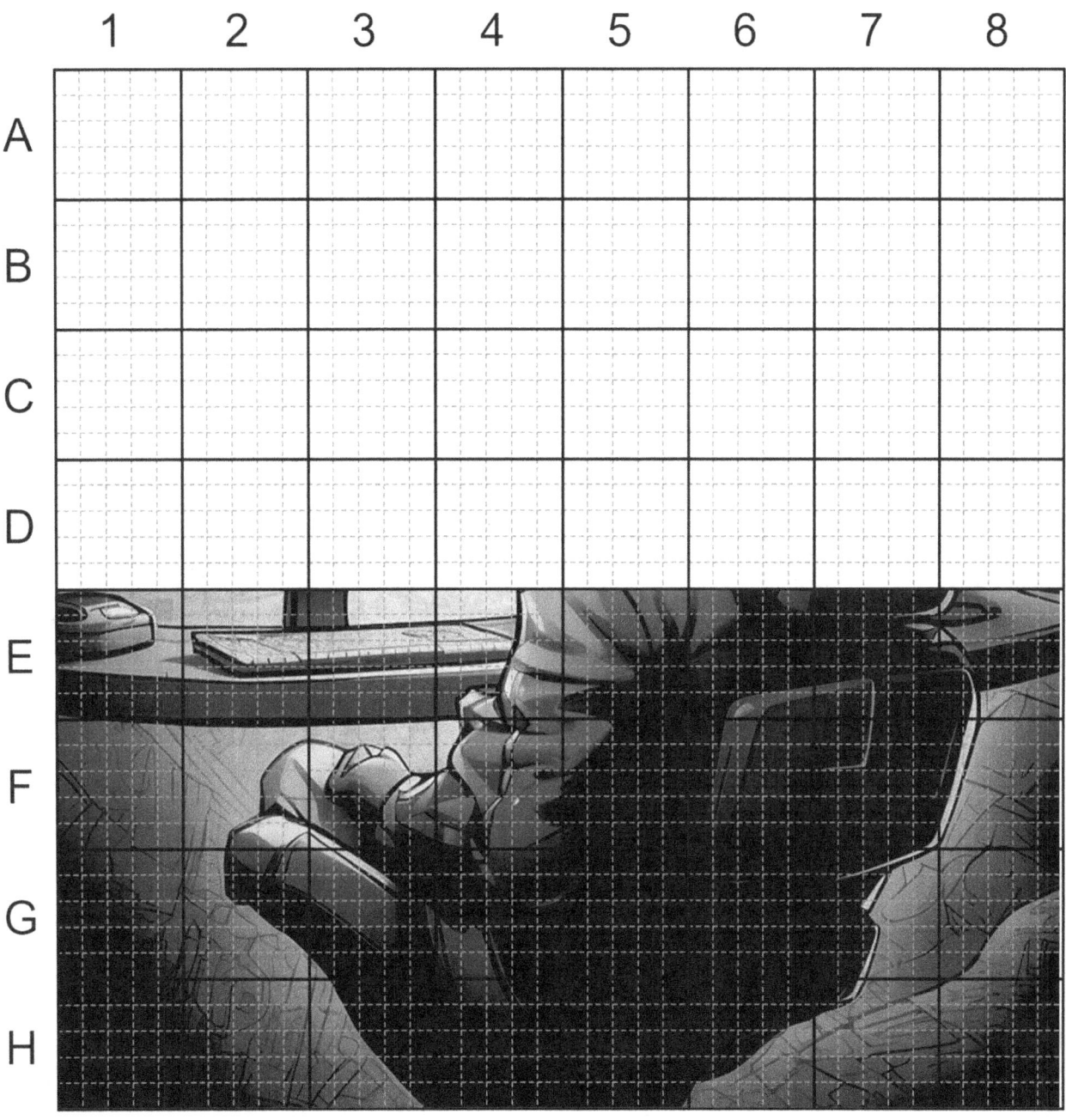

FINAL PICTURE

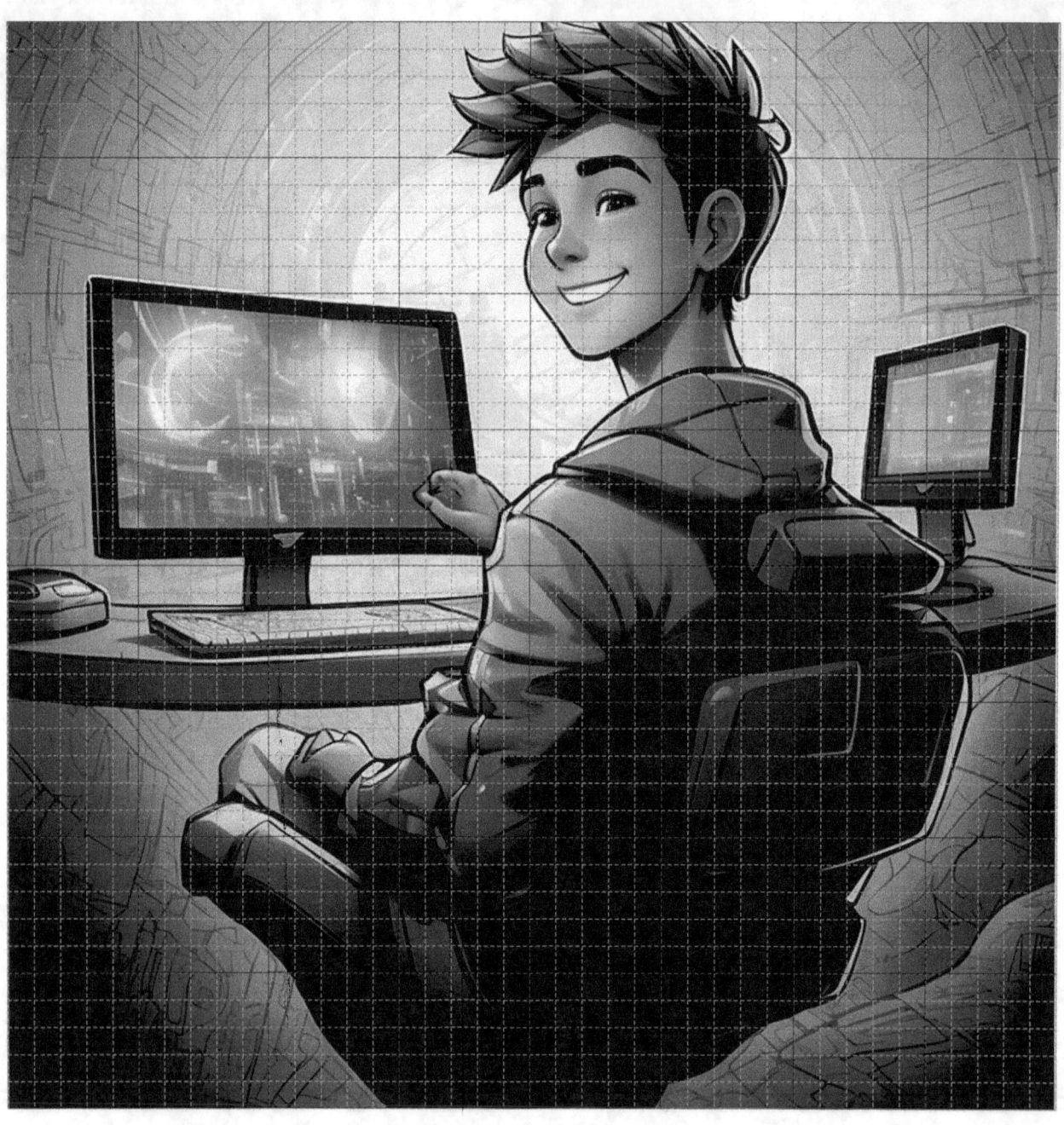

www.ingramcontent.com/pod-product-compliance
Lightning Source LLC
Chambersburg PA
CBHW081116240526
45470CB00020B/3296